THREE SURNAMES AND A JR.

Memoirs of Logan Napier Muir Jr.

Ruth C. Muir

Printed in the United States of America.

ISBN: 978-1-4269-3938-9 (sc)
ISBN: 978-1-4269-3939-6 (hc)

Library of Congress Control Number: 2010912050

*Our mission is to efficiently provide the world's finest, most comprehensive book publishing
service, enabling every author to experience success. To find out how to publish your book,
your way, and have it available worldwide, visit us online at www.trafford.com*

Trafford rev. 10/15/2010

 www.trafford.com

North America & international
toll-free: 1 888 232 4444 (USA & Canada)
phone: 250 383 6864 ♦ fax: 812 355 4082

For Andy and Al

Preface

In this volume the author has gathered together newspaper clippings, pertinent letters, and other memorabilia of Logan's life. Many of these events are relevant to his professional career; others occurred within our family.

In the back of Logan's mind was always his parents' families in Scotland. They lost touch with Bob Waugh, his mother's brother, after WWI, and Logan knew only that Uncle Bob came to the United States and that he liked horses. When Logan's profession took him around the state he always checked in the telephone directory for his Uncle Bob. Finally a picture in the local newspaper featured him as he registered his thoroughbred horses for races at the California State Fair. Logan learned that Uncle Bob had been living only a short distance from us for many years.

Late in his business career, Logan could finally go to Scotland for the first time. We walked around an Edinburgh neighborhood and he said, quite simply and from his heart, *"I feel as if I've come home!"*

Logan began writing his life's story late in life and completed only two pages. The author continued his story in this book. She hopes she has done justice to him by referring once again to the serious and humorous episodes that help to flesh out the true story of this professional man who never forgot his humble beginnings.

Acknowledgments

Special thanks and gratitude to our two sons, Andy and Al, who took on responsibilities beyond their years. Their presence enriched the daily lives of our family in too many ways to count.

Contents

Introduction: The Royal Muirs

[Logan wrote the following paragraphs when England's Princes William and Harry were still wee lads.]

The Royal Muirs
By Logan Napier Muir, Jr.
Scots are justly proud of their line of Stewart kings and queens— and why not? After all, the present royal family of Britain are direct descendants of that line. But little recognition is given to the fact that all royal Stewarts excepting the very first one are descendants of a Muir!

The Stewarts gained their name from Walter fitzAlan, Steward of Scotland under Robert Bruce of cave and spider fame. Known as King Robert I, Bruce had defeated the English led by Edward II at Bannockburn, near Stirling, in 1314. His daughter, Marjorie, married Walter and their eldest son Robert succeeded to the throne of Scotland, becoming the first of the Stewart Kings when Bruce's only son, King David II, died childless in 1371 ..Robert II had succeeded his father as Steward under David II and as regent while David was young and during later absences. Sometime during this period, he married Elizabeth Muir (Mure) although, because of difficulties with the Pope around that time, their marriage was not sanctioned by the church and therefore not considered legitimate however, in 1349, after relations with the Papacy were healed, the marriage received sanction. The first child of their union was a boy, born in 1340 and named John, though after the death of Robert II, the name was changed to Robert and he ascended the throne as Robert III. There followed a long convoluted story of a series of Jameses, I through V, all descendants, father to son, from Robert III. James V died in

Falkland Palace on December 14, 1542, only six days after the birth, in the palace of Linlithgow, of his only surviving child, Mary. On September 9, 1543, the nine-months old babe was solemnly crowned at Stirling Castle as Mary Queen of Scots. To understand the descent to the present royal family, it is necessary to note that James IV, Mary's grandfather, had married Margaret, the eldest daughter of Henry VII of England, thus also establishing Mary as a direct descendant from the Tudor line in that country. It is also noteworthy that Mary Queen of Scots also became Queen of France for a short period by her marriage to Francis II, though there were no children by that marriage. Eventually, there was a child, James, born in 1566, by her marriage to Lord Darnley, a cousin and also a Stewart. James eventually became James VI of Scotland and, on the subsequent death of the "virgin" Queen Elizabeth I, James I of England, in 1603.

There followed in succession the reigns of Charles I and II which were rudely interrupted by the Cromwells with the beheading of Charles I. James II, second surviving son of Charles I and brother of Charles II, was next as King of Great Britain and Ireland, but was eventually forced to abdicate to be succeeded by the joint reign of William and Mary. William, of the Netherlands, was the son of Mary, daughter of Charles I, and in addition had married another Mary, the daughter of James II. Another daughter of James II succeeded William and Mary as Queen Anne. Upon the death of Queen Anne, a great-grandson of James I from Hanover in Germany succeeded to the throne of Great Britain as George I. From George I, there is direct descent to the present Royal Family.

It is almost certain that if a Robert Muir had married an Elizabeth Steward that Scots would celebrate the Royal Muirs rather than the Royal Stewarts.

So if anyone says you're a "moor-dweller" wi' grass twixt your taes, just tell them there's guid Muir bluid in all thae kings and queens o' Bonnie Scotland since Robert I, and all thae kings and queens o' Great Britain since Elizabeth I, richt don tae wee William and Harry! Here's tae us — wha's like us!

References:

Crowl, Philip A., The Intelligent Traveler's Guide to Historic Scotland, Congdon and Weed, Inc., New York, 1986

Encyclopedia Britannica.

Fraser, Antonia, Mary Queen of Scots, Delacorte Press, New York, 1970.

MacLean, Fitzroy, A Concise History of Scotland, Viking Press, New York, 1970.

Prologue—April 22, 2002

John Anderson my jo, John
We clamb the hill thegither,
And monie a cantie day, John,
We've had wi' ane anither;
– Robert Burns

This life in the 20th century began with Scottish immigrant parents struggling to find opportunities in the new world, and ended with unexpected recognition. The author feels uniquely favored to have been a witness and participant in that life, which brought challenges, friendship, and devotion to the 65 years since their first meeting. Now, more than eight years after his death, the life they shared is as vivid as if he had been at the breakfast table this morning.

*   *   *   *   *   *

As I prepared food in our modest kitchen Logan sat in the living room where I glanced his way occasionally. When preparations neared completion, I announced, *"Breakfast will be ready in six-and-a-half minutes,"* or however long the estimation was. Logan looked up from his crossword puzzle, acknowledged with a wave of his pencil that he heard me, smile, nod, and prepare to get out of his chair.

Now in his late 80s, he was cautious and deliberate with everything. He needed extra time to wash his hands and make his way to the dining table, reaching for a wall, a chair, a table for stability as he went. When the food was ready, so was he. Each meal began with a bear hug. Sometimes we came close to toppling over as we forgot, in the fervor of the moment, to brace ourselves.

On the last morning of his life, we repeated this breakfast ritual, followed as usual by a cut-throat Scrabble game. We played as if high financial stakes were involved, since only something truly earth-shaking could interrupt our thoughtful deliberations. Of course, the stakes in this case <u>were</u> high: our daily game kept us mentally agile even when the rest of the body clearly was not. However, we never thought of it that way—it was simply a good time we anticipated and shared.

After Scrabble our morning included a walk outside to find something interesting. It was a gentle walk with time to observe the new buds forming on trees or bushes, and a chance to use his new walking stick. The stick itself was wrapped in black leather, and on top was mounted a beautiful engraved knob with the same Navy insignia seen on a naval officer's hat. It brought a smile when he talked about it. The stick had more status, he liked to say, because it was not called a cane. Besides, it cost more. He never forgot his humble struggling beginnings when the prudent use of money was of utmost importance.

Logan didn't just happen to be a man of unswerving morality who found ways to keep life exciting through dreary times. Sometimes events fashioned his outlook. Often he found or created his own opportunities.

Thirteen days before he died Logan began his hand-written memoirs. Without being able to include details that only Logan would know, I will attempt to flesh out the story of this dependable man, who had an aura of confidence, but never thought of himself as remarkable. What he wrote a few days before he died is only two pages long.

I was born on July 6, 1914, so I can only give my views of the 20th century for the latter six-sevenths of it. But six out of seven ain't bad, so here goes. Life for me started in Chicago, Illinois, at the Norwegian-American Hospital. My father was born in Edinburgh, Scotland, January 2, 1882, in a tenement at No. 3 Potterow which is now a part of Edinburgh University. My mother was born on September 2, 1888, in Bathgate, Scotland, a village approximately halfway between Edinburgh and Glasgow. Thus, my Scotch blood is neat, although some native Scots feel that since I was born in the U.S.A. it is somehow diluted. To peg the time of my birth to other major developments: WWI started on August 4, 1914; the Panama Canal opened on August 15,

1914. In my early years, I remember there were many Union Veterans of the Civil War. Their group was the G.A.R., or Grand Army of the Republic, and they paraded on patriotic holidays.

One of my earliest recollections—I must have been about two years old—is of my father taking me to one of Chicago's city parks—Humboldt, I think. Although a working class man, he was dressed in a blue suit, white shirt and a tie. As we sat on a bench, he reached into his jacket pocket for some peanuts which he then tossed one by one toward a nearby squirrel, with each toss bringing the squirrel a little closer. Eventually, the squirrel hopped up on the bench and when he saw the source of the peanuts was my father's coat pocket, he reached in to help himself. I thought this was marvelous and that my father was the most wonderful man on earth!

Incidentally, my mother and I, and eventually my two brothers, always called my father "Pa", and he shall be so called in the rest of this account.

CHAPTER 1—EARLY DAYS
Six-Sevenths of a Century

Whose little body lodg'd a mighty mind.
– Alexander Pope

When the author first met Pa about 1940, he looked like many other American working men of that time: small and muscular. His body was toughened by years of shoveling coal from the train's tender into the locomotive firebox. His speech was spare, but what he said was meant to be heard. Pa was not fooled by my vacant smile as I strained to make sense of his Scottish dialect, but someone was usually nearby to interpret for me.

Logan Muir [senior] arrived in New York on May 10, 1907, aboard the *SS Furnessia*. The manifest in 1907 lists him as a butcher. He might have learned this in his military service during the Boer War in South Africa and it is probably what drew him to Chicago. For many years Chicago's stockyards were the terminus for the herds of cattle raised on the great plains states to the west. Surely Chicago would present opportunities for a butcher, he thought. But at that time parts of the city seldom saw the sunshine, and the fetid stockyard smell penetrated large areas of Chicago. It was best not to be downwind.

At that time Upton Sinclair's fictional book, <u>*The Jungle*</u>, was being recounted with shameful abhorrence as it exposed to the whole country the unbelievably unsanitary—and often cruel—working conditions in the meat-packing plants. Largely because of this book, a stockyards act was passed in 1906 which provided for federal inspection of meats shipped in interstate commerce. But the regulation did not cover meats shipped within state lines. It is possible that the working conditions in the meat-packing plants turned Pa away from butchering.

Meanwhile, the Hepburn Act of 1906 provided some regulation of the railroads. Pa soon recognized a more desirable future in that field. By the time of his marriage in 1911 he was a fireman for the Chicago, Burlington, & Quincy R.R. operating out of Chicago.

In the 1920s much of the country was having a rousing good time with no care—wasn't the raging stock market wonderful? Everyone had money to spare, it seemed. Yet those were the most difficult years for the Muirs. At first they lived in a flat on 63rd Street in Chicago. Pa was on the"Extra List", which meant he would be called to work only when the railroad needed him. Pay was sporadic at best.

One day their two-year-old second son, Dave, wandered to the front gate, waited for someone to come by, and then said, in his clear but incomplete vocabulary, *"Open 'a door 'a me, Mon!"* The man obliged, opened the gate, and let Dave out. This alarming incident alerted Ma and Pa to the urgent need to move out of Chicago.

They chose the village of Clarendon Hills, 18 miles west of the city and on the CB&Q Railroad. In that country village their young boys could run free. On the edge of town was an acre of gently rising land, with a swale across the front. The land looked ideal, but it had no house. However, a neighbor had a sturdy old barn for sale. The Muirs had it moved to the top of the little hill where it became their home. Before winter they covered it with tar paper, and that's the way it stayed during the 1920s. By any standards it could be referred to as nothing more than a shack.

A railroad fireman's job was all physical: hour after hour of shoveling coal into the locomotive to keep it running. In summer the heat of the fire was almost unbearable. In winter it was almost unbearable too, as one side of the body was seared with burning heat from the firebox, while the other side was chilled with icy cold from the open tender. But a job meant money to support the family, and it had to be done.

Pa took pride in his work and left home each day wearing immaculately clean and pressed overalls. He lit a corn-cob pipe with long stick matches as he walked the mile to the railroad station. According to neighbor Rob Raisler (one of Logan's elementary school friends) more than once the fire department had to put out a fire started in the tall grass by one of his discarded matches.

The CB&Q "Extra List" provided employment, but it often meant long hours. A law that prevented railroad employees from working more than 8 hours without a break was neatly—and legally—circumvented. Often Pa arrived home exhausted from shoveling coal for 8 hours, slumped down at the table to a nice hot meal, and the phone rang. It was the Railroad telling him of a fireman's job available. He had to return to work. How could he refuse? He had a family to feed. He hoped also to establish seniority. At some point in the '20s Pa was promoted from fireman. On his naturalization papers his profession is listed as "Engineer".

Pa's routes took him through Clarendon Hills, and it was 12-year-old Logan's responsibility after school to deliver a hot meal to his father when the train stopped at the station. One day as Pa reached down for the dinner pail, he grabbed Logan's arm and pulled him up into the locomotive. The startled wide-eyed youngster rode the 10 or 15 miles to Aurora and back in the cab.

"Keep your head doon when we go thr-r-r-ough toon so the station moster won't see you!" Pa warned.

Seeing his father operating the machinery, hearing the bells and whistles, smelling the coal burning, and watching the towns pass by from high in the cab all left indelible impressions on the young lad. Logan's love affair with trains lasted all of his life. Yet it was the demands of this hard job that made Pa say later, without hesitation, "No son of mine will work for the railroad!"

There was little cause for humor in that struggling household, yet it seemed to fill the nooks and crannies of the converted barn and dispel dreariness. It was humor, not mockery, in Pa's obervations when he referred to Mr. Barrens as Mr. Bare Knees, and Mr. Sehstadt as Mr. Haystack. A local man of some importance was Orrin P. Goode, and one need not go far to uncover the fun they had with the grammatical error in that one. Very likely without intention—it was simply his way with words—Pa sharpened the perceptibilities of his three young lads.

As Pa trudged through the railroad yards in Chicago, he sometimes came across an abandoned baby animal whose mother had been sent to the stock yards. Occasionally, Pa brought an orphaned animal home if he thought it wold make a good pet for his growing sons.

One day he arrived at the front door with a young billy goat. Logan and Dave enjoyed sparring with the goat, and took turns grabbing his tiny horns and wrestling him to the ground. When not playing with Logan and Dave the goat was tethered in the yard to nibble the tall grass.

Yards in the village were not fenced and people commonly short-cut across them for convenience. One such person was the neighborhood Bad Boy who crossed regularly to buy milk at the store. This was no problem, except when the billy goat was tethered there. Bad Boy seldom missed an opportunity to pelt the goat with stones as he passed through. With confident calculation he stood just outside the radius of the tether and waited expectantly as the goat ran full tilt toward him. When the goat got to the end of his tether, he was pulled up short with a jerk and tumbled to the ground. Bad Boy thought this was hilarious and enjoyed it again on the way home with the milk.

On one of Pa's rare days home he chanced to witness this developing scenario from the kitchen window. While Bad Boy was at the store, Pa stepped outside, quietly untied the tether, and the goat continued munching grass as usual. On his way home Bad Boy threw the stones as before and laughed as the goat started toward him. This time the angry goat didn't stop. The Boy, the milk, and legs and arms seemed to fly in all directions. Tears and surprise overwhelmed Bad Boy but the Muirs watching from inside the house knew that Pa's direct approach had solved the problem.

Ma and Pa were strict disciplinarians and Logan learned responsibility early. One day while his two younger brothers were fighting in the back yard Logan was in the front yard, uninvolved. Suddenly Pa stormed around the corner of the house and, without a word, boxed Logan's ears. *"You're not supposed to let your brothers fight!"* he scolded. There was no room for explanations or disagreement. I asked Logan much later if he was angry with his father over this. *"Of course not,"* he said withooout rancor. *"I knew what I was supposed to do."*

One day Logan had to use all the tact a young lad could muster. He had done some naughty thing or other that boys sometimes do. Pa shook his head as he scolded, and finally sighed regretfully, *"You should have known my father. Now there was a man!"* Logan pondered this briefly. He liked and respected Pa, and came up with his own opinion: *"He couldn't have been half the man my father is!"* Pa turned this over in his mind for a moment, and then his stern face melted into an appreciative smile.

Pa's long hours meant he could seldom spend time with his boys. But at home Ma was unwavering in her oversight of their young family – as we shall see in another chapter.

CHAPTER 2—ALEXIS
A Nice Cup of Tea

Like strength is felt from hope, and from despair.
— Alexander Pope

When Logan's mother, Alexis, was elderly and forgetful I visited her each week in the nursing home where she had the care she required. She seldom recognized me, but with long-standing affection and mutual agreement I addressed her as "Lex". She was courteous and seemed to enjoy my presence. More than once she thought I was someone from her long-ago past.

One day when I visited her, Lex was one of several patients slumped in their wheel chairs just outside their rooms. A maid approached down the hall with a bucket and cleaning supplies. She stopped near Alexis to pick up a scrap on the floor. With her back turned, she didn't see Lex put on an impish smile and a wink, point her toe, and give an imaginary kick in the direction of the Maid's derriere.

This was only a minor interruption in her on-going ramblings to people I didn't know, about things I had never heard of. Her voice never became frail like the rest of her body, but when she lowered it to a soft whisper I pricked up my ears. Expecting to hear something of real importance, I listened as she addressed 'her friend from long ago' and said, *"I nearly died when I saw the scrawny thing Logan was going to marry!"*

This incident became a treasured family joke, and Lex would have laughed harder than anyone, had she understood to whom she was talking. It did illuminate one of her viewpoints: scrawny was not desirable. Plump was a synonym for good health and prosperity, and Alexis was plump as long as I knew her.

Logan had been a frail lad and she invented gimmicks and games to coax him to eat. Sliced carrots became nickels and dimes; prunes were something you ate so you could count the prune stones. Years later, when Logan returned from Trinidad, Lex was happy to say that he had become "a stylish stout". I told Logan that perhaps she had over-coaxed.

Ma grew up in the town of Bathgate, Scotland, about half way between Edinburgh and Glasgow. Her father did a bit of celebrating when she was born, but managed to register her as "Alexica" on her birth certificate. Scots were known for shortening or changing their names to suit themselves, regardless of what the birth certificate said. For practical purposes her name was shortened to "Alexis", a name already in the family. She was the second eldest in a family of three girls and three boys.

When she was 17 her mother was expecting a seventh child and there was no extra room in their crowded house. Margaret, the eldest child, was expected to leave home but refused to go, so it fell to Alexis, next in line, to leave. Arrangements were made to go to America with her Aunt Jessie. Nevertheless, Alexis had a good friend in her father, who said if she ever wanted to come back he would pay her fare.

It is unclear whether Aunt Jessie went to Scotland expressly to pick up Alexis, or whether it was one of her regular visits from Chicago back to the "Auld Sod". At any rate their ship, the _Carthaginian_, arrived in New York from Glasgow on October 1, 1905, after a 13-day voyage. It would be more than sixty years before Alexis returned to visit her native land.

Before her marriage in Chicago Alexis worked for a couturier named Frenchie, whose specialty was fashioning the big picture hats in vogue in the early part of the century. Alexis already knew how to sew and crochet. From Frenchie she picked up valuable dressmaking tips. *"Don't make the inside perfect,"* Frenchie said. *"It's the outside people look at!"*

Much later, during WWII when two sons were in unknown places exposed to unimaginable dangers, she completed a table runner with a message subtly crocheted into the pattern: *"In God we Trust"*. It was a simple solemn expression from her heart.

Alexis had been a diligent student in Scotland and could quote Shakespeare or Robbie Burns or a range of other classical authors as appropriate. She undoubtedly inspired Logan to read widely. Her welcome at the front door was always a straight-faced, *"Come in if your feets' clean."* Her soft Scottish dialect was easy to understand and her speech was much like "the King's English".

Alexis remained a British citizen all her life. She was a young teenager in Scotland when she became a "White Ribboner" and pledged that she would never let liquor cross her lips. Occasionally she proudly wore the tiny white ribbon emblem. Some might slyly try to trick her in a weak moment into breaking the pledge, but Alexis would not be swayed. Her serious side said firmly, *"No! I took the pledge!"*

Alexis and Pa met at the Caledonia Club in Chicago. It was where Scots kept alive the memory of Robbie Burns, Sir Walter Scott, haggis pudding, gathering of the clans, bagpipes and other things Scottish. They were married July 3, 1911, at the Woolley Memorial Methodist Episcopal Church on Indiana Street.

Alexis often said the happiest time of her life was when the boys were small. When Logan was a toddler the small family still lived in Chicago. She often took him on the streetcar, and as it rocked from side to side, little Logan clutched the seatback and quickly got into the swing of things. With a mother's confidant incite, Alexis happily said, *"He thought he was causing the swaying and jolting."*

One wonders how those early years could have been so happy, given the circumstances of this immigrant family. After moving out of Chicago, their home was a former barn, tar-paper covered, in Clarendon Hills. Pa worked uncertain hours and often slept days while the three growing boys had to be absolutely quiet if they played in or near the house. Water for bathing and washing was hand-pumped from a well in the back yard. Drinking water was brought from a neighbor's property—one of the regular chores for the boys as they carefully toted big buckets of it on their wagon or sled. Electricity had not yet reached their house, and wash days represented unbroken labor from morning until night.

Alexis's good nature was sometimes tested on the weekly washday. It was a time for slaving in the basement, scrubbing clothes on the washboard, heating water on a coal burner, and generally working up a good sweat over it all. Interruptions in the routines were not welcome. When she heard a knocking on the front door upstairs, she ignored it. Probably one of her boys wanting something, she thought. For Alexis, nothing was more urgent than getting all those dirty clothes clean.

When the knock was repeated with persistence, she impatiently yelled upstairs, *"What the h--- do you want now?"* She was mortified to hear the minister's voice respond! As she later retold this story Alexis would throw back her head and laugh, and always ended with the reminder that you have to be able to laugh at yourself.

Alexis could laugh at herself

It was up to Alexis to make ends meet, and sometimes they didn't. Fortunately, Mokel's Grocery let them charge foods they needed to carry them over, if necessary, until Pa got paid again.

During the summer months, a half-acre of their property became a vegetable garden. A farmer was paid to plow the land in the early spring, and the family did the follow-up work of breaking up the clods, and raking and smoothing the fertile soil. Pa helped when he could with planting, and the three boys did their share, pulling weeds down the long rows of corn or beans or tomatoes. On summer evenings they each took a small empty jelly jar, put a bit of kerosene in it, stepped carefully through the potato patch examining the leaves as they went, and dropped hungry potato bugs into the jars. They all knew a good potato crop from their garden would be a staple on their table for months to come.

When garden produce was ready to pick, Logan and Dave–and perhaps also young Bob–took it around town in a kid's wagon, peddling it from door to door. Sometimes Mokel's would buy their choice corn or other fresh vegetables to sell in their store. In this way Ma and the boys earned a few extra pennies for the family. Spare coins from this enterprise were dropped into a ceramic parrot hanging prominently on the bare wall.

The Muir's had a chicken coop for their well-cared-for chickens. One of Logan's chores as a kid was to clean the chicken coop each week. This meant shovelling, chipping, and scrubbing, summer and winter. On cold winter mornings, when the temperature dropped below freezing, Alexis made a hot mash to warm the chicken's insides. Thoroughness was necessary—it's what made the chickens a treat. Occasionally a Mokel customer would request one of Muir's chickens if she were giving a special dinner party.

Ma believed in rewarding the family when she could. Near the end of the month when Pa's wages were all spent, the parrot money helped tide them over until payday. If any coins were left they all had a treat, perhaps even ice cream.

Disciplining her sons was part of being their mother. Her caring attitude toward them was tempered by the conviction that she was raising them to be "pushed out of the nest", as she so often described it. She was the mother bird who taught them to fly, and after that they were on their own.

The land on which the tar-paper covered barn stood had been uncultivated, and between the barn and street was a wide swale. Alexis knew it would improve drainage and appearance if it were filled in a bit. And the household throw-aways needed a place to be thrown away. Assorted trash included the occasional tin can, and anything else that would disintegrate. This is where she buried an old bed spring, carefully covering it with dirt hauled one wheelbarrow load at a time from a high spot on the lot. She was thorough and careful about everything she did, and, if pressed, would tell about the bedspring, but there was no braggadocio—it was simply hard work that had to be done. When I walked across the beautiful lawn with her some years later, she said, *"Would you believe there's a bed spring under here?"*

After the barn was remodeled into a house in the 1930s Alexis rewarded herself with a flower bed on the west side. Her favorite flower was the Oriental poppy—too beautiful for words, she said— and when the bloom opened, all she could say was *"Oh!"*

When I first met the family in the early 1940's, the re-modelling had been completed. The immaculate house was sparsely furnished. A picture had been put into a frame and hung high on the living room wall. The scene might have been from a calendar that was particularly enjoyed, or perhaps it was a picture cut from a magazine.

Their conversations were like their home—without excess ornamentation. What was spoken had a purpose that made it important. Why else would one bother to say it?

Alexis always liked winter because it gave her time to put her feet up, study colorful seed catalogs and plan for the growing season ahead.

But summer or winter, she did like a nice cup of hot tea. She made it according to the Scottish way: "hot the pot" with boiling water for a few minutes, pour it out, put in the loose tea leaves and boiling water, and finally cover the brewing tea with a tea cozy to keep it hot and delicious till the last drop. Loose tea leaves in the bottom of the teacup fired her imagination and as she scrutinized the bottom and tilted the cup a bit, she made little noises: "Hmm… Aah!…Oooh…." that had no relation to real words. She saw birds flying, or clouds drifting, or ships sailing. All seriously announced, of course, but somehow we all knew it was just good fun.

After Pa died she left Illinois and came to California to be near us. Logan was the eldest son and it was no burden to him to take the responsibility of caring for his mother. It was then that our friendship flourished. We walked in the mall together, drank tea together and had time for conversations. When her dresses were being fitted, she always mentioned her sloping shoulders, which she compared to some ancient queen who also had sloping shoulders.

Alexis always believed it was better for women to have a little mystery about their attire. If a young, scantily dressed woman passed us in the mall, Alexis continued walking as she swung her worn black purse back and forth. Her eyes followed the short skirt, but she did not bother to lower her voice as she said with dismay, "*Would you look at that!*"

With three sons one might expect her to have a favorite. In later years when she lived with us, her son Bob often telephoned to stay in touch. Their conversation always began something like this: "*Ma, this is your favorite son!*" Her reply was always stern, always the same: "*I have no favorites.*" No laughter. No hint of a smile. At the other end of the line there was a big guffaw—Bob knew that, in spite of his teasing, what she said was true.

In 1966 at age 77 Alexis was finally able to return to Scotland for a visit. Her mind was drifting a little, and she needed a bit of watching, but a later chapter tells of the trying incidents engendered by her failing memory and a reunion.

Eventually she put all of her assets in joint ownership with me, rather than with any of her three sons. I knew it was merely a temporary accommodation so that I could pay her assorted bills when she could no longer do it herself. I am honored that in her mind I had come a long way from the scrawny thing Logan married.

CHAPTER 3—ELEMENTARY SCHOOL YEARS
Be Kind to your Fine Feathered Friends

'Tis education forms the common mind:
Just as the twig is bent the tree's inclined.
– Alexander Pope

In 1920 the Muir family still lived in Chicago. Logan attended first grade at Earle School at 6121 South Hermitage Avenue. A class picture shows 31 first-graders, but no more than three smiles—a serious group indeed. Undoubtedly the squirming six-year-olds were sternly lectured on the need to stand very still while the photographer handled the long film exposure necessary for a good picture. Logan spoke of Earle School only as his first school, with no mention of events or the teacher.

Logan's youngest brother Bob was born that year, and it must have been crowded in the flat at 1754 West 63rd Street. In 1921 the family moved out of the city to Clarendon Hills.

Dana Bailey was a young friend of the Muir family in Clarendon Hills. He became a Rhodes scholar, a noted astronomer, and an expert on bristle cone pines, among other distinguished accomplishments. When Dana died in 1999, the following excerpt is from a letter Logan sent to Dana's sisters at that time. The letter pictures life in the little village of Clarendon Hills.

> *...I thought some reminiscences of Dana might interest you and the end of the century would be a good time to recount them. My family moved to Clarendon Hills in 1921 at which time I was in the second grade. The following year, I believe, Dana started school–two grades back of me at that time. My brother, Dave, and a neighbor boy, Robert Raisler, were in that same class and my association with them probably brought me in contact with Dana. Also, the*

Bailey house was on Eastern Avenue which was on the route from my house to the R.R. station, P.O., and village stores, and we were bound to meet in our goings and comings. Anyway, Dave and I, Dana, Ed Hirsman, and Rob Raisler, all living on the south side of the R.R. tracks, formed a club, as boys will, which we called RMBH. The capital letters we derived from the last names of the participants. My mother made us a flag out of a piece of an old sheet with RMBH in red letters cut from other fabric, sewn on in an arc. We had a code: RMBH-1 through -5, the latter, RMBH-5, being our distress call. If a member were ever threatened, he had only to holler, "RMBH-5", and presumably the others would come to his assistance. Fortunately, this was never tested, but there was a certain comfort in having it! The other numbers were for meetings, alerts and other related activities.Rarely did all five of us do things together. Usually it was some combination of three or even two. Your mother was very watchful of her children—Dana had to come home for a nap every afternoon, much to our chagrin, and his too, I imagine. He was forbidden from going to Johnson's Slough, a shallow lake of about 10 acres or so located on farmland about a quarter of a mile back of my house, where the rest of us would go to swim or fish in summer, or to skate and sled in winter. On occasion, he would accompany some of us as far as my house and stay there with my mother, either chatting or doing a cross-word puzzle. Frequently during the latter, he would call on her for help, and she would give him the appropriate word. Finally, he would toss the puzzle in the air and declare, "Another puzzle done without any help from anyone!"But he joined us in other activities. Flagg Creek was just across the street from your house. It had a variety of water plants and even little minnows. We used to race objects, we called them boats, in the current. Across Flagg Creek and up the hill was Hamill's hay barn. When loose hay was stored there, we would do somersaults from the rafters. Sometimes the hay was in bales and we would re-arrange the bales to provide tunnels and rooms.   Dana particularly enjoyed roaming the fields and it was on these excursions I learned a lot about plants and butterflies from him.   One meadow had a heavy population of a butterfly called a 'fritillary.' Another was covered with blue gentians in their season and we called it 'gentian field.'

Of course, we hungry boys roved the area for apple trees, pear trees and the big cherry tree in your yard. On summer nights we could chase fireflies and, when tired of doing that, look skyward where Dana could always point out and name the constellations…

With so much freedom to roam the town and swim in Johnson's Slough as often as possible, it's natural that curious young lads would get into trouble occasionally.

One cold winter day Logan and friends went to Johnson's Slough after school to find out if the ice was hard enough for skating. The ice broke away under their feet and they were dunked into the frigid water. The boys did the only sensible thing that boys would do at that time: they built a bonfire to dry out their coats and hung them on the branch of a nearby tree before taking them home, where there might be a lot of explaining to do.

It's uncertain where they got the matches, but the fire succeeded in warming the boys more than the coats. Finally, when it was time to go home, they discovered their coats were frozen stiff! Not wanting to face his mother with this bit of news, Logan quietly sneaked into the house and hung his coat downstairs near the furnace. As Robbie Burns once said, *"The best-laid schemes of mice and men gang aft agley…"* This one was no exception. Logan forgot the report card in his coat pocket. The teacher expected it back tomorrow with a parent's signature on it, but the slough had blurred Logan's grades beyond readability. Logan never went any further in this tale, but there must have been a bit of explaining to do.

Another young friend was Bill Goletz, though their association began as adversaries. Logan's boyhood is pictured in this part of a reminiscence sent to Bill's widow upon his death in 1991.

BILL'N ME

It must have been about 1926. The country considered itself prosperous under President "Silent Cal" Coolidge. But then as now the less affluent were not that much touched by it. I was 12 years of age and living in a tar-paper covered house at 57 Sheridan Avenue near the southeast corner of Clarendon Hills, Illinois, a middle-class suburb eighteen miles southwest of Chicago.

The adjacent suburb to the east was Hinsdale, a somewhat larger town, such that it could boast of a second rail depot on the Burlington that bore the sign, "West Hinsdale." Bill Goletz lived in West Hinsdale. His modest home was about two blocks east of Jackson Street, the boundary between our two towns, while mine was a long block to the west. Thus, in the open spaces existing there at the time, we were virtually neighbors but since each town had its own schools, Bill and I did not know each other.

In those days schoolboys had "clubs", a less threatening term than "gangs". Our Clarendon Hills club, RMBH, consisted of Rob Raisler and his younger brother, John; myself and younger brother, Dave; then Dana Bailey and Ed Hirsman. On Bill's side there were their leader, a big fellow for his age, Al Brokoff; Fred and George Klinke, and maybe one or two more whose names I can't recall. We called them the Brokoff Kids, and we only were aware of them from some distance.

Now, you were no more able to have two boys' "clubs" representing adjacent towns be at peace then than you are today, and one fall afternoon as some of us were climbing pine trees just west of Jackson Street, we were pelted by stones from sling shots coming from the West Hinsdale side. A couple of us had "BB" guns and ran home to get them. Upon returning, we peppered a lattice shed in which Brokoff Kids had taken refuge, and dodged the return fire of stones. The skirmish lasted maybe ten minutes when survival overcame valor and each side slipped back deeper into its own territory.

Occasionally, there were other similar conflicts. Looking

> *back, I'm a little ashamed of using a "BB" gun. Though spring-operated and not as powerful as today's air gun, they were dangerous and the only mitigation is that the stones from the sling shots could be dangerous too...*

At the Clarendon Hills Elementary School three grades occupied one classroom, with 8 or 10 students in each grade. Miss Durland was capable and perceptive for the thirty or so pupils in her 6th, 7th, and 8th grades. Music, art, and outdoor field trips combined all the classes in one activity; but arithmetic, grammar, spelling, history and geography were taught at each grade level. For Miss Durland this meant 12 to 15 different lesson plans and recitations each day, plus the combined activities. Each student provided his own books, pencils, pens, ink, paper, and other supplies as needed.

A lunch for the entire classroom was prepared by a different mother each day, and brought to class steaming hot to nourish the growing bodies. In addition, a mid-morning break gave them an opportunity to buy a half-pint of milk (5 cents) and a graham cracker. The minimal school library was augmented with a rotating supply of fiction and non-fiction books personally selected by their teacher at the city or county library.

Logan remembered the music classes fondly. Miss Durland would crank up the phonograph and play a recording of a classical musical selection. The students were to guess the title or the composer, or sometimes the instrument featured. The compositions were wide-ranging and especially appealing to young minds. "*The Grand Canyon Suite*", or "*Clare de Lune*", or "*The Swan of Tuonela*", all with strong visual images, were favorites.

Logan laughed as he recounted the singing lessons, when he and some of his creative classmates found ways to be inventive. With the entire room filled with song, their fractured lyrics were not acknowledged by the teacher. But what sly fun those boys had. To John Philip Sousa's Stars and Stripes marching song, instead of "Hurrah for the red, white, and blue", they sang:

> *Be kind to your fine feathered friends,*
> *For a duck may be somebody's brother.*

Miss Durland clearly liked children, but might have been hard-pressed at times to keep ahead of their inventiveness.

The pupils always looked forward to their field trips. These were outdoor neighborhood walks to identify the birds and plants shown in full color in each student's bird- and plant-books.

The standards for reading, writing, and arithmetic were high. By the time he finished 8th grade, Logan had read most of the books available in the school library. At home he had read the entire *Old Testament*. His parents subscribed to the *Saturday Evening Post*, and he read parts of it, particularly the continued adventures of a youth his age, which left the reader eagerly waiting for the next issue. At graduation ceremonies Logan gave the valedictory. He was well prepared for the challenges and opportunities he would encounter in high school.

CHAPTER 4—HINSDALE HIGH SCHOOL
A Post-Graduate Course

Hope springs eternal in the human breast,
Man never is, but always to be, blest.
– Alexander Pope

In 1928 Logan's thoughts focused on a new problem that was developing in his perceptive mind. The skirmishes with the BB guns were behind him. However, he would be attending high school in the neighboring town of Hinsdale, and would likely be forced to cross paths with some of his old adversaries there. His anxiety and its solution weighed on his mind, and were contained in part of this letter written some 70 years later. It was sent to Bill Goletz's widow when Bill died:

> *… Sooner or later, after graduating from grammar school,*
> *I was going to be confronted by big Al Brokoff and his Kids*
> *on their own turf.In the fall of 1928 I enrolled in the high*
> *school and kept a wary eye open. Fortunately, I could board*
> *a train at the Clarendon Hills depot to get to the main*
> *Hinsdale station and on to school, thus avoiding crossing*
> *"enemy territory" on foot. Both Al and Bill Goletz were a*
> *year older than I, so I was able to avoid them successfully.*
> *Fred Klinke was a freshman, too, but I don't remember*
> *seeing much of him. I don't know exactly how it came*
> *about, but I was confronted by Al Brokoff in a corridor*
> *one day. To my great relief, he just grinned at me and said,*
> *"Those were some battles we used to have, weren't they?"*
> *Now that the veil of fear was lifted, I began to walk from*
> *my home to the school, a distance of about one and a*
> *quarter miles, and occasionally I'd meet Bill or Fred or*
> *both and we'd walk together, to or from school. Nothing*
> *was ever said about the "battles".*

> *Eventually Bill graduated and then a year later, Fred and*
> *I, followed by George a year later...*
> *As I look back, I remember* [Bill] *as one of the kindest,*
> *gentlest men I ever knew and I'm proud that he had*
> *considered our continuing contacts to be worthwhile.*

Logan's first day at Hinsdale High School is best described by his life-long friend whom he met that day. They quickly became acquainted, because their names were adjacent in the roll. It's likely that Logan was the trigger for this incident.From Brockway McMillan, upon learning of Logan's death... :

> *I first met Logan in Miss Blaisdell's English class on the*
> *opening day of our entry into Hinsdale Township High*
> *School, to which Logan "commuted" from Clarendon*
> *Hills. Seated alphabetically, we were side by side. In*
> *ten minutes, we were laughing so much that Miss B. was*
> *forced to separate us. For the 74 years since, in his presence*
> *and in memory, I have enjoyed Logan's zest for life, his*
> *unfailing sense of the ridiculous, and his sardonic, albeit at*
> *heart sympathetic and humane, view of the passing scene.*
> *I continue to cherish those memories...*

Hinsdale was a comfortable community of middle-class residents. Some of Logan's classmates had leisure time to learn the fine points of a golf swing or take ballroom dancing lessons. A few students even had their own cars. The high school set high academic standards and the teachers prepared their young charges well to succeed at whatever university they might attend to complete their formal education. With Logan's early background of reading almost everything he could get his hands on, he fit in easily with this group and made the most of his time there as he relished the opportunities available.

Between classes he put extra minutes to use. While other students tarried or the teacher took the roll, he opened his books and completed the homework for the class just finished. He knew there was little opportunity to study at home after school–too many chores were waiting. Never once, during his four years at Hinsdale High School, did he take home a text book to study.

By the time Logan was in high school, he had developed a practical viewpoint to his decisions. He walked a mile-and-a-quarter to and from school each day, morning and afternoon, and repeated the same to go home for lunch, all of which added up to more than five miles daily. He reasoned, therefore, that it was unnecessary to take PE, and with the informality of the PE roll-taking, the coach didn't miss him. In order to have time to go home for lunch, however, Logan also ditched his first afternoon class, a study hall. This, too, went on for some time until he was missed. Miss Brickbauer, the vice-principal, was sympathetic toward this good student, but kindly and firmly insisted that he attend all of his assigned classes.

There was one more practical touch to this story. With homework finished, Logan and a friend had to be separated in the library where they had found a corner to play chess during study hour.

By this time in his life Logan was used to dealing with all sorts of adversity, and was not one to let a problem get in the way of a solution. One wintry day the snow was especially deep, transportation was at a standstill, and, if there had been advisories in those days, people would have been told to stay home. But Logan doggedly trudged through the drifts to school, arriving at the principal's office at 10:00 A.M. to pick up a "late" slip. Half the students were absent and the astonished staff told him he should have stayed home on such a terrible day.

During his senior year Logan passed the Morse Code key test and fulfilled all other requirements for the Amateur Radio Operator's License. He and his friend Brockway spent spare time on their radios, at first only "talking" to each other on their home-made radio sets. When atmospheric conditions provided good reception, Logan expanded the miles of his transmissions into global communications.

With each successful global CQ, Logan sent his printed card with his call letters, W9IPP, his address, and a few words about the quality of the reception. The mail soon brought return cards from far away, and the farther the distance his transmission was heard, the greater the delight. He began to think in terms of the entire world, and searched the atlas for these new countries.

When the Hinsdale High School class of 1932 had its 30th reunion, Logan was unable to attend due to business commitments. But he sent a lengthy note, one small part of which reads as follows:

… Tell Scott Jones that I shall always remember his generosity, and think kindly of him because of it, and I think he'll remember why…

Here is the "why". Caps and gowns were not yet in use for high school graduations, and the dress code for commencement in Hinsdale included white pants for the boys. White pants? What could Logan do with white pants after graduation was passed? He didn't mention this to his parents. He knew they could not afford a pair of white pants for only one occasion. Some class members were sympathetic, and Scott Jones was one of several students who offered to loan him a pair. With his usual determination to stand on his own two feet, Logan chose to miss graduation ceremonies rather than accept the well-intentioned offers.

He graduated 11th in his high school class of 77, and might have been higher except he possibly remembered when his younger brother David graduated from 8th grade.

A year after Logan was named 8th grade valedictorian, the school board was faced with the prospect of naming Logan's brother David to that same honor. In its "wisdom", however, the Board deemed it unfair that the valedictorian should be from the same family in consecutive years. They named someone else (perhaps equating it with a popularity award), and the unfairness of *their* decision did not occur to them. In Logan's perceptive mind the pursuit of scholarship and honors might have lost some of its luster at that time. Circumstances and events were different later, but after 8th grade he never again attended a graduation ceremony.

In 1982 Logan was retired and able to attend his 50th Hinsdale High School class reunion. He happily said he was being hugged by girls he scarcely dared to look at when he was in school!

The following is a retrospect from Ruth's Trip Diary:

We arrived in Logan's hometown on a Thursday in order not to miss a minute of the three days of week-end festivities planned for his 50th high school class reunion. A brief drive around town told us we hardly recognized Clarendon Hills, as former landmarks had all but disappeared into a suburban maze of sidewalks, gardens, and homes. Even Johnson's Slough where Logan swam and

played as a kid was now expanded into beautiful Ruth
Lake with an adjoining country club.
At early Friday breakfast in a local coffee shop, seven young
people slid into the corner table near us. Their conversation
drifted back and forth between giddy and serious, and it
was easy to overhear that they were all graduating seniors.
We quietly enjoyed their conversations as our thoughts
turned back to fifty years earlier. With breakfast finished,
Logan walked over to their table and introduced himself.
"Do you want to know something?" he asked the group in
general. "In fifty years you'll look like me," and he pointed
to his white hair. Egged on by their cheerful convulsions of
laughter, he continued. "…and you," he pointed to one of
the girls, "are going to have six kids." More convulsions.
They were a courteous group and one asked eagerly, "Did
you go to Central High?"
"Central High? There was only <u>one</u> high school when I was
here; and it served <u>two</u> towns!" They continued comparing
notes about each others' school days.
Finally Logan leaned over to one of the boys and in an
audible whisper, said, "Do you know we used to skinny
dip in Ruth Lake?"
"You couldn't have!"… "You've got to be kidding!"… "Not
really!"…and assorted other exclamations came from the
laughing group.
"Of course it was called Johnson's Slough in those days.
There wasn't a house in sight. Only fields as far as the eye
could see."
And with that bit of historical up-date we parted company
and went on to the reunion, invigorated by this real-life
flash-back provided by young people who were exactly fifty
years younger.

When Logan graduated from high school in 1932, the depression was
being felt by more and more people and one of the popular songs of the
day was *"Brother, can you spare a dime?"* Almost everyone knew these
words by E. Y. Harburg:

*Once I built a rail-road, made it run,/ Made it race
against time./Once I built a rail-road; now it's done; /
Brother can you spare a dime?/Once I built a tower to the
sun,/ Brick and rivet and lime./Once I built a tower; now
it's done /--Brother, can you spare a dime? /Once in khaki
suits,/ Gee, we looked swell, / Full of that Yankee Doodle-
de-dum. / Half a million boots went sloggin' through hell;
/I was the kid with the drum. /Say, don't you remember,
they called me Al? / It was Al all the time. /Say, don't you
remember, I'm your pal! / Buddy, Can you spare a dime?*

Men waited in long bread lines, or stood on street corners selling apples for a dime in order to buy a bit of lunch, or to help pay the rent, or just to keep their self-respect. Job openings were almost impossible to find. A new high school graduate had few opportunities to find paying work. College was never an objective for Logan. His immigrant parents knew nothing about educational opportunities beyond high school, and for some reason Logan did not know about the University of Illinois' scholarship program in effect at that time.

On a selected day in spring the University conducted academic tests in each Illinois county. All high school seniors were eligible to compete, and each county was permitted three scholarship winners. The top scoring applicant could choose any major; the next highest man received an agriculture scholarship; and the next highest woman, a home economics scholarship. The scholarships covered all tuition and matriculation fees. Even had he known about the test, Logan might not have taken it, because the additional expense of room and board at the University would have been prohibitive for him.

Without a job available, Logan returned to high school for a post-graduate year. He took a math course because he liked math and wanted to learn more; and another course, possibly public speaking or typing, to improve his job skills. After completing the post-graduate school year in 1933 he was presented with a job opportunity by someone who undoubtedly knew of his dedication to doing anything well if it was worth doing at all.

CHAPTER 5—THE PORTLAND CEMENT ASSOCIATION
Engineers Were Not Washing Dishes

Love seldom haunts the breast where learning lies,
And Venus sets ere Mercury can rise.
– **Alexander Pope**

Strangely enough, as the depression continued during the 1930s and many families struggled financially, the Muir family began to prosper. Pa was taken off the Extra List and was finally given a locomotive engineer's job on the Burlington commuter trains between Chicago and Aurora. Perhaps even more important, this meant a regular payday. And with Logan's post-graduate high school course finished, he obtained a job which was menial but paid well for a beginner.

This beginner's job was offered by Brockway McMillan's father who worked for the Portland Cement Association (PCA) in Chicago. Logan was given the opportunity to start at the bottom by washing beakers and other laboratory equipment. It was not ordinary dishwashing–the chemical tests conducted by the PCA followed the strictest standards of cleanliness, thoroughness, and accuracy. The cement industry was guided by the results of those tests and there was no room for carelessness or indifference. But he did have a job, a status especially valued in those days of high unemployment.

His pay was about $60. a month--very good for a high school graduate with little experience in those times of bleak opportunities. Out of this he gave his mother a fair amount for room, board, and laundry, and bought himself respectable clothes for commuting on the railroad. He also saved a bit with no particular objective in mind except he knew all about "rainy days" by experience, and didn't want to be caught without an umbrella.

Another employee in the lab became his mentor and showed Logan the fine points of preventing breakage: *"If something starts to fall, get your foot out under it to break the fall.*" This and other practical wise advice served him well more than once.

Bill Goletz, formerly of the "Brokoff" gang, was a fellow commuter when Logan worked at PCA. Here is another part of the letter Logan sent to Bill's new widow in 1990:

> *...by 1933 we* [Bill, two friends, and Logan] *had jobs in Chicago...Bill with Continental-Illinois Bank and I at the Portland Cement Association. I don't remember where the others worked. We all caught the 7:24 A.M. train from the West Hinsdale depot and occupied facing seats. We each bought the morning <u>Chicago Tribune</u> which we would read, commenting at times about this or that news item while ogling around the open pages of the paper as some pretty girl got on at LaGrange or Riverside. And what dudes we were! Felt homburgs, suits, ties —the works, including brief cases. I don't know what the others carried in their brief cases, but mine had my lunch in it...*

Logan worked 44 hours a week, the same as most other men who were fortunate enough to have jobs at that time: eight hours Monday through Friday, plus four hours on Saturday mornings. Saturday afternoons were free time and he often went to Wrigley Field to root for his favorite baseball team, the Chicago Cubs.

The son of the Cubs' president was Bill Veeck, Logan's high school classmate, and occasionally Bill and Logan rode the train together between Hinsdale and Chicago. Bill knew everything about Wrigley Field. Among other beginning jobs, he helped plant the ivy on the famous ivy wall in the outfield. With that jump-start in the baseball world, Bill eventually became the owner, at various times, of the Cleveland Indians, the St. Louis Browns, and the Chicago White Sox. Over the years Logan occasionally sparked up conversations with baseball fans by reminding them that Bill Veeck was the owner who signed a midget in 1951. When the midget came to bat, the fans were in an hilarious and appreciative uproar, and the midget was walked in his only time at bat.

In 1962 Bill Veeck's book, *Veeck as in Wreck,* was published. It was also the year of the high school class's 30th reunion, which Logan could not attend. But he sent a letter to the reunion with this acknowledgment in it:

> *Bill used to twit me about what would happen if the irresistible force hit the immovable object. I told Bill* [on his birthday card], *and I'm sure you'll agree, that he is the irresistible force but that an immovable object has not yet been found that's a match for him…*

The noon lunch break at the Portland Cement Association was a welcome change from Logan's beaker-washing. Sometimes he swam at the nearby YMCA. Many times he walked out on Navy Pier, bought a hot dog and a bottle of root beer and took in the action on the lake front. There was time to think about his future and assess his own talents.

He was quick to observe opportunities which the educated engineers had at PCA. He thought night school courses at Northwestern University might help him get ahead, and in 1936-37 completed a 4-unit course in Elementary, Analytical, and Physical Chemistry. He wasn't sure how this would fit into his future, but he saw that the engineers were not washing beakers.

One night after attending late classes, he stepped off the train at Clarendon Hills about midnight. The full day of work and classes had left him drained of thought. He tried hard to keep from stumbling. The route home was across the tracks and to the south. The rest of the way would be easy—every intersection, every curb, every crack in the sidewalk on the way home was familiar.

At that time the CB&Q had three tracks through Clarendon Hills: outbound from Chicago, inbound, and a center rail for high-speed through trains going either direction according to tight schedules.

After his train pulled out Logan started across the tracks. His exhaustion kept him from hearing the whistle of a train bearing down on the center rail. The gust of wind from the speeding train jolted his brain from its stupor and shifted his balance. It was a startling incident, one not soon forgotten, which he later wove into one of his successful story assignments.

At home in the 1930s things were going better financially. Pa was taken off the Extra List and was given a regular commute assignment as an engineer. The railroads had no central dispatcher as now, yet timing of each and every train was critical. In order that each engineer's watch was accurately set and dependable, it had to be taken to a particular jeweler to be checked for accuracy once a month. The engineer's timepiece was a crucial piece of equipment on the train, and the engineer's ability to stay on time—speeding up or slowing down as needed—was of supreme importance for accident-free performance.

Logan regularly rode the 5:24 p.m. home, which also happened to be Pa's train. Before departure Pa leaned out of his cab to watch for Logan, and they exchanged waves as Logan boarded. The 5:24 left Chicago on the center fast rail, and as it neared the suburbs it switched to the outgoing track, a maneuver that slowed the train almost imperceptibly. Still, all the regular passengers knew where this slowing would occur and accepted it routinely. Some used it as a signal that they neared their stop; others gauged how many more minutes until they, too, would get off.

One day as the train neared the switch, Logan didn't detect the slowing. He thought to himself, *"My God! Pa's forgotten!"* But just on time the train slowed and smoothly switched to the outgoing rail. It reinforced his opinion of Pa: he was one of the best locomotive engineers. He knew precisely the engine's response and how to give his passengers a smooth ride. Even in retirement in 1948, Pa was selected to put those honed skills to use in Chicago's Railroad Fair.

Gradually as Logan's responsibilities increased at PCA he was entrusted with tests involving cement. When the tests were completed, any remaining unused cement was discarded. With permission from his boss, he poured this leftover concrete into a form to make one stepping stone at a time. As each one finished curing, he carried it home where, altogether, they made a handsome path from their front door at 57 Sheridan Avenue to the street.

Alexis always sent Logan to work with a good breakfast under his belt. She was the first one up each day to start the routines. One morning she shook Logan awake.

"Logan! Get up! I've overslept! You'll miss your train!" and they each hurried to do in minutes what usually took an hour or so. Finally, while Logan ate breakfast, someone thought to check the clock and discovered that Ma had mis-read the time when she was only half-awake. It was 3:00 a.m!

Logan's diligent work at the PCA did not go un-noticed by the management. One day he was called into the office and was asked, *"How would you like to go to college?"* Logan knew little about college, but did know that it cost money and that a college education opened new opportunities. He admitted that he probably couldn't go unless he could earn some money at the same time.

The Portland Cement Association often dealt with the Testing Laboratory at the University of Illinois, and Mr. H. F. Gonnerman sent this letter in June, 1937:

Professor Frank E. Richart
104 Materials Testing Laboratory
University of Illinois
Urbana, Illinois

Dear Professor Richart:
You will recall that some months ago I mentioned to
you that Mr. Logan N. Muir of our laboratory staff
is planning to enter the Engineering College at the
University this fall. Mr. Muir is anxious to obtain work
during his spare time so that he can earn part of his way
through school. It would be greatly appreciated by both
Mr. McMillan and me if he could obtain work in your
department in the Materials Testing Laboratory. You may
be interested to know that Mr. Muir has been employed
by our Research Laboratory since his graduation from
high school in 1933. He started work in our Chemical
Laboratory and soon became very efficient and skillful
in carrying out work assigned to him. In recent months
in order to give him a broader understanding of our
various test methods and procedures we have had him
assigned to different jobs, such as freezing and thawing
tests, making mortar and concrete specimens, and volume
change tests. He also will become thoroughly familiar
with the operation of our testing machines before he
leaves for school. The training which Mr. Muir has had
will be of great help to him in case he obtains work in

> *your laboratory. He is a very conscientious worker, pays attention to details, and keeps his eyes open for any unusual phenomena that may develop during the course of the test. I am sure that you will make no mistake in giving him employment in case you have any work available which he is qualified to fill. With best regards, I am*

> *Sincerely yours*
> */S/ H. F. Gonnerman*

In the 1930s President Franklin Roosevelt laid out a number of different plans to get the country out of its deep depression. Congress passed acts to support and create, among other projects, the WPA (Works Progress Administration), the NRA (National Recovery Act), and the NYA (National Youth Administration). Detractors called them alphabet soup, but they did provide employment, with a starting wage of 35 cents an hour. Most University departments, including the Talbot Laboratory, had a few such employment opportunities for students. Because Logan had a relevant work history, he was offered an NYA job with a starting hourly wage of 50 cents. His "rainy day" savings and this job would pay for tuition, lab fees, books, supplies, and room and board.

With the recommendation from Mr. Gonnerman, Logan told his girl friend of his new opportunity. Her reply was, *"If you really love me, you won't go away to school."* Hearing that admonishment, Logan knew immediately that he and the girl had no future together. Logan saw a better life ahead. Mr. Gonnerman was opening a door for him, and he could scarcely imagine what was on the other side. In early September, 1937, this 23-year-old, unencumbered, left for Urbana to find the answer.

CHAPTER 6—THE BOARDING HOUSE
Straightening Out a Silly Sophomore

For he lives twice who can at once employ
The present well, and ev'n the past enjoy.
– Alexander Pope

In the mid-1930s the ratio of men to women students enrolled at the University of Illinois was about three to one. Maria—'i' as in 'pie'—Maria Leonard was Dean of Women and kept a guarded watch on her young charges. Hundreds of women students were housed in several women's residence halls near campus, each with a strict housemother who enforced Maria's rules. The first floor provided living room and dining space. Men were not allowed upstairs which was for the women's studying and sleeping quarters. Evening study hours were by the clock. At 10 p.m. all visitors downstairs had to leave and the dorm doors were locked, with an extension of a few hours on Saturday nights. Off-campus accommodations for women were also rigidly regulated. Only women students living at home were exempt— their parents would provide the necessary oversight. But Maria's name was always used with awe, affection, or dismay, depending upon the circumstances.

Men students, on the other hand, had no late-night restrictions and were free to come and go according to their own schedules. In their rooming houses, study hours were voluntarily enforced by mutual consent. Many Champaign-Urbana families offered their spare bedrooms to students, and it was common to see signs in front windows, "Rooms for Rent–Men", or "Rooms for Rent–Women". A few homes also offered meals.

The Reverend Frederick O.Claussen and his wife Emma headed one such family in Urbana. In 1936 three of their offspring were attending the University. To off-set the costs of higher education, they opened a men's rooming house on Elm Street with optional meals. Their eldest son was completing his doctorate at Oxford

University in England and their second son would complete his doctorate in physical chemistry in several years. He would live upstairs with the roomers, while the rest of the family, including their second daughter, a University sophomore, squeezed together downstairs. Their location was particularly convenient to the engineering buildings on campus.

In early September, 1937, Logan went to Urbana to take care of remaining enrollment preliminaries. His walk from the Urbana-Lincoln Hotel in downtown Urbana to the campus took him past 611 West Elm Street where he saw the "Room for Rent–Men" sign. He knocked on the door expecting to get some idea of what was available. The sixtyish gentleman who answered the knock showed Logan the choice of accommodations and they had an interesting first chat. Rev. Claussen was comfortable talking with—and drawing out—people of all genders, nationalities, and backgrounds, and Logan liked this elderly gentleman immediately. It was an easy decision for Logan to rent the front bedroom upstairs, the best room in the house. He also decided that "Rev. Claussen" was too cumbersome a handle, so he dubbed him "Mr. C.", a name that stayed throughout their friendship. He liked his wife, too, because of her gentle manner and she, of course, became "Mrs. C." The charge would be $30. a month for room and board. Logan always liked to add an important facet to the story of their first meeting: *"He didn't tell me that he had three daughters!"* Those two people whom he liked immediately were my parents, and I didn't meet Logan until some time later, probably at the dinner table. I was the youngest in the family, a fourteen-year-old silly sophomore in Urbana High School.

With accommodations arranged and a job ensured at the Materials Testing Laboratory, Logan moved to Urbana and registered at the U. of I. He used his rainy day savings, plus his earnings at the Lab, to pay for tuition, lab fees, books, and room and board. It was "cash and carry", and he bore all expenses. There was little money for extras, but by watching his pennies he might chip in with other roomers to buy a pitcher of beer occasionally, or indulge in some other treat.

Logan as a freshman at the University

One of Logan's first challenges was an impromptu quiz by his professor of advanced trigonometry who wanted to determine early in the semester how much his students knew and whether they were doing their assignments. Logan looked at the page and couldn't read the questions. He knew what the problem was: he needed glasses. Finally, he handed in a blank paper which of course was returned with an "F".

On the next quiz Logan's "A" puzzled his professor who called him into his office for clarification. Ever straightforward, Logan simply explained the new glasses. The professor tore up the first quiz in front of him.

Logan always functioned best in the morning. He was often up before the other roomers, and completed a theme or other assignment during the fresh start of a new day. He skipped classes that, to him, seemed unimportant. Tennis students in PE were on their honor to put in time on the court. This was easy. He was already a good tennis player with a wicked back-hand—I found that out later by experience—and with a like-minded opponent in the class, they flipped a coin to determine the winner. But the instructor discovered the ruse, and gave the coin-flippers D's.

Logan saw right through the motives of the student who had not studied, yet engaged a professor in long-winded explanations when the answers were in the text. He paid another roomer to occupy his assigned seat in a huge lecture hall, while he spent his time in a more practical way earning money or studying. In this way he balanced his decisions, pitting intellectual need against financial practicality.

Logan studied diligently, and had an insatiable curiosity. Yet he knew there was more to life than engineering. Before he graduated he completed 20 units of non-engineering courses in philosophy, short story writing, advanced narrative description, public speaking, English writers of the 19th century, and sociology. He suggested that I, too, should take courses outside my major in order to broaden my interests. He continued his membership in the "Book-of-the-Month Club", and loaned me several volumes to read: *Anthony Adverse* (2 volumes); *Wind, Sand and Stars*; and Carl Van Doren's biography of *Benjamin Franklin*. He did well in his rhetoric classes, and ended a book review of Van Doren's' book by comparing reading to a garden for the mind, which needs watchful cultivating. His final sentence in the review was, " *I must go now and tend my garden.*" I was impressed with the clarity and originality of his writing. But I was not alone in this assessment.

At that time the English Department had a campus publication called, *The Green Caldron*, which contained the best examples of good writing by freshmen rhetoric students. The best of those and a few relevant others were combined into a hard cover book, *Student Prose Models*, by Professors Charles Roberts and Leah Trelease. It became a text book for freshman rhetoric classes. Logan's theme, a composite based loosely on the idiosyncrasies of several of the roomers at 611 West Elm Street, was included under the heading, "Descriptions of People". It spotlights Logan's ability to organize thoughts clearly and understand different viewpoints—traits that served him well throughout his life.

TONY WADDELL
Logan Muir

(...to the Dean of Men)
Dear Sir: With this letter I wish to introduce Anton
Waddell, one of our graduates of last semester. I was Tony's
English instructor during his senior year in Maklin
High School, and because of this contact I believe my
understanding of him is correct. Tony is an easy-going,

gentle boy with an honest love for beauty in nature, music, and art. A tendency toward tardines, procrastination, and 'dreaminess' is merely the outward manifestation of a bona fide creative ability. He has an undeniably attractive and half-humorous manner of expression both in his speech and in his written work. His work as a member of our poetry club and his drawings for our last year book are proofs of his ability. Last semester he composed a song which, while never completed, was not inharmonious.

Here is a boy who, with proper understanding and sympathy, should go far.

God speed him!

Sincerely yours,

Cecilia Watts

(…from his roommate)…and Ma, this roommate of mine is the limit. The other chaps in the house are more than anxious to take him apart to see what makes him do the things he does. On St. Valentine's Day, he had no money to buy flowers for his girl, so the boys said they would give him a dollar and a half in advance if he would walk downtown and around the main block in his pajamas. And he did it! The night before last, the boys tried to put some ice down his back, but he scurried up a tree—took to the tall timber, as it were—and stayed there for two hours. When he came back he had written quite a number of poems in his pocket notebook. He is forever going about in a daze, and is apparently quite thoughtless of the other fellows. He will leave the hot water running till it's all gone; he sings and whistles late at night and early in the morning; he kicks open doors so as not to get germs on his hands; and he slams them shut again with his foot. I really like the kid and I try to straighten him out, but he just forgets everything I tell him. Well, Ma, guess I'll try to get some rest now. So long, and love to you and all the family. Charlie

(...to a friend in the college town)

*...and as Tony's mother, I am quite worried about him
being away from home. I am somewhat consoled by the
fact that his association with other boys will be profitable,
but I am frightened to think they will be a little hurtful.
Tony's father died, you know, when he was six years old,
and while I have done everything I could to teach him and
bring him up, I do realize that he lacks a father's strong,
strict love and influence. I know Anton Waddell would
have supplied just that. Oh God bless them both!*

*Won't you please drop in and see me the moment you
arrive in town?*

*Nothing would make me happier right now than to see
you again.*

Your affectionate friend,

Ruth Waddell

A series of study questions followed in order to help the student explore the fine points of the description. For many years we had two copies of this book in our family library. One was Logan's complimentary copy from the authors, and the other was the text book I studied later in my freshman rhetoric class. It would not be the only time for me to read carefully something Logan had written.

Sunday evenings at 611 West Elm Street found the family and some of the roomers gathered in the living room for supper on trays, while everyone listened to the radio and laughed at Jack Benny or Edgar Bergen and Charlie McCarthy. After supper, some of us played Chinese checkers or Parcheesi, or put together jig-saw puzzles. The real wizards played chess and took winning or losing seriously. Occasionally the chessmen and board became air-borne by an unhappy loser. All-in-all, it was an uncomplicated, happy week-end regimen, and it left the roomers ready for the tough challenges which they knew they would face in their studies in the week ahead.

Better be a nettle in the side of your friend than an echo
—**Ralph Waldo Emerson**

During those early U. of I. years, I was merely an observer from a distance of this new boarder, as he was also of me. Early one cold wintry morning he glanced out of his upstairs window and happened to see me leave for school without a scarf. He had two and promptly gave me one of them. I began to take notice of this man who showed a new side that I had not seen before. I noticed also that my mother liked him because he paid his rent on time and often settled disputes among the roomers upstairs. My dad liked him because he was someone with whom he could have a serious discussion. I began to think of him as a brother, except he never teased. Probably the most impressive side, for me, was that he didn't fawn over me. The youngest child in a family is often spoiled, and I was no exception. My parents and four siblings thought everything I did was wonderful. It had its roots in my early medical problems, but it was a relief to find someone who scolded me when necessary or straightened out my thinking.

One such event occurred when I had a big disagreement with my mother. Since I don't remember the cause, it likely was trivial beyond compare. This teen-ager was right and she was wrong—that's all there was to it, and I was mad at her and the world. I got on my bike and rode as far and as fast as I could straight out of town. Later, when I unburdened myself to Logan (my "brother") and told him I hated my mother, he said,

> "*Why would you hate your mother? She cooks for you, she washes your clothes, she wants you to get a good education, she picks up after you. Why would you hate her?*"

I had no answer, but his unthreatening voice displayed genuine concern. He began to loom as a man with logic in his speech and actions—logic that this teenager had never before noticed. Perhaps later it was this incident that caused Logan to say, often in a light-hearted manner, that he raised me from a pup.

The world was unsettled during Logan's years at the University. The radio brought international problems into our living rooms. Hitler was becoming a fearful driving force. When British Prime Minister Chamberlain came back from Munich in 1938 to declare Hitler wants "peace for our time", the world breathed a little easier.

But the respite was short-lived, as Hitler gobbled up Poland and ran rough-shod over any country in his path. In 1939 England and Germany were finally at war, and the tension in the United States increased. Intervention and isolationism were loudly heard in all quarters, and each side was adamant in its stance. Because ours is a democracy, America's course was not clear. On the minds of every University student was the probable conscription of men for military service. The reality of such a draft, which would also affect able-bodied men of college age, made for heated bull sessions in the rooming house. There were no demonstrations on campus—students were more determined than ever to concentrate on completing their educations, and no one had time for demonstrations.

During Logan's junior year, one of his roommates was Clark Burton, who was petrified with the thought of going to war. He found a way to defer that fearful event by training as a pilot somewhere in Kansas. He hoped the war would be over before he became licensed. We learned later that he did complete his training, but was killed in a flying accident before leaving the states. Everyone was at risk, it seemed.

Industry was gradually shifting its manufacturing toward war materiel, at first only to be sent to England as part of the Lend-Lease program. Logan's mother sent a few pantry staples to her sister Nell in Scotland, to ease the strict rationing they endured. Talk of war was everywhere.

In June, 1940, all but the last of the Claussen children had completed their higher educations, and with the generous assistance of some of the older siblings my parents were able to close the rooming house and buy a small, comfortable home in east Urbana. It was newly constructed, and Mr. and Mrs. C. were enchanted with their new surroundings. That September I enrolled as a freshman in the University and Logan began his last year there.

With the rooming house closed, and his employment by then in the public works offices of the city of Champaign, Logan needed a new place to live. One of the city's requirements was that he be a Champaign resident. My mother and I wanted to help her favorite roomer find a suitable location. Somewhere about half-way between downtown Champaign and the engineering campus would be ideal, giving him access to his job and to his studies. One such rooming house was near the Illinois Central railroad tracks, and Logan immediately found it to be the perfect place. Being close to the railroad was an added bonus.

The engineering buildings were north of Green Street and my freshman classes were to the south. I knew all about the exacting demands of the senior curricula from my brothers and sisters, and in addition Logan worked long hours to pay for it all. I thought perhaps we would seldom see each other. But on Wednesday afternoons we both eked out a few free hours from full schedules of work and classes. We met on the campus broadwalk under the elm trees at 4 o'clock to go for a walk. Always we found things to talk about, and always he lent encouragement to me in my studies. Sometimes we walked much farther than we realized.

One such long walk took us to West Champaign, and it was nearly dark before we turned back to the campus. When he saw me to the bus that would take me home, I noticed the bright lights of the new Student Union Building. It was the day of the grand opening, with people going in and out and admiring the new patio area. I was not aware that my parents watched my growing interest in Logan, and I did not tell them why I was late getting home. All I knew was that the new Student Union Building was a useful excuse for my tardiness.

Logan's senior year included a course in water supply. Each student was assigned a particular nearby city for which he was expected to design a proper water supply solution. Logan's assignment city was Monticello, Illinois. From practical experience he knew the most logical place to begin would be in the Monticello Public Works Office. The engineer in charge there was delighted to show Logan what they already had. Expanding upon that basis Logan designed a new system, more up-to-date to accommodate new technology, current conditions, and expected community growth. He had an architect friend design a beautiful structure to house elements of the new system. This became the cover of the report. All of these things he would have done in proper sequence if this were a real-life job. He knew that this project was the culmination of a semester's work and his final grade would weigh heavily on it. He was pleased and satisfied with his presentation. However, his professor was not. The report was returned with a grade of "C". At a conference with the professor Logan simply explained that this is what he would do in real life. The professor's ego took a sharp blow when he finally had to admit that the student had actually done a creditable amount of proper analysis. The professor reluctantly gave him a grade of "B" for the semester.

During Logan's senior year at Illinois he was interviewed for a number of jobs. In early spring the Eastman Kodak Company flew him to Rochester, New York, for an interview. It was a posh way to travel in those early flying days. Though we had no understanding about marriage or our future, he casually asked me how I would like to live in Rochester. It seemed to me that he was thinking seriously about "popping the question". However, mine was a close-knit family, and Rochester was a long way from Illinois where most of my family lived. I couldn't imagine living far from all of them. Logan sensed my hesitance. He correctly understood that I was not yet ready to make such an important decision.

Great Britain had been at war since September of 1939, and as events unfolded in Europe, the U.S. watched with disquietude. The most likely threat was that Hitler would cross the Atlantic with his U-boats and use his terrible aggression in the Western Hemisphere.

Much has been written about the unity of the American people during World War II. But events leading up to the declaration of war in December, 1941, found the country far from unified. Charles Lindbergh, who was idolized and revered by Americans for his historic solo flight across the Atlantic, was a noted isolationist. Some people thought he should be president. Senator Burton K. Wheeler of Idaho was an outspoken isolationist critic of President Roosevelt. He spoke eloquently against the Lend-Lease Program under consideration by Congress.

The war was going badly for Great Britain and their resources were being stretched to their limits. Clearly, they needed some kind of help. Our own national borders were deemed vulnerable. A lend-lease program under consideration by Congress would give Great Britain 50 U.S. destroyers. This would help Britain's defense. In return, they would allow the U.S. to have 99-year leases of certain of their Crown colonies in the Western Hemisphere. This act would strengthen our position in the world, and the bill did become law after the usual heated debates. The details of the Program were yet to be worked out.

As Logan's graduation neared, this new law presented him with a different job opportunity. The Crown colony of Trinidad, British West Indies, with the U.S.'s recently acquired 99-year lease, was selected as a site for an air base in defense of the Western Hemisphere. Professor J. J. Doland of the University's civil engineering department was asked by the government to go there in June and get the job started. Choose two graduating engineering students to accompany you, he was told. He hand-picked two seniors, Ken Compton and Logan Muir. In Logan's mind the offer of a job in Trinidad sounded interesting, partly because of his Scottish roots and this would help Great Britain's war effort. He recalled that as often as possible Ma sent packages of sugar and other staples to her sister Nell in Scotland, where all citizens were under extreme rationing restrictions of ordinary foodstuffs.

Further, Logan had an almost uninhibited curiosity and joy in adventure. He could imagine living in a foreign land, eating native food, exploring the terrain and customs, and being paid for it! It was an opportunity Logan readily accepted.

A small newspaper clipping (of unknown origin, but possibly the Champaign-Urbana *News Gazette*) tells of their departure:

> *When Professor J. J. Doland, College of Engineering, civil engineering department, arrives Monday in Washington, D.C., he will meet Kenneth Compton and Logan N. Muir, Jr., both graduating from the University this month. They will not remain for commencement, however, because of summer Appointments.*

> *Professor Doland leaves here Sunday. The trio will meet at the office of the division engineer of the eastern division of Washington, reporting to Colonel J. D. Arthur. Compton and Muir will get their appointments for work with Professor Doland in the Trinidad district in connection with construction of bases on various islands of the group. They sail June 12 from New York. The seniors didn't learn until Thursday they were to get appointments. Then they heard by calling Washington. Headquarters will be maintained at Port of Spain, Trinidad. These islands have been leased to the U.S. by Great Britain as a site for military bases. Professor Doland expects to return September 12.*

Never one to find much sense in the black gowns and tasseled caps of commencement exercises, Logan missed those ceremonies in 1941 without regret. By the time those festivities took place in Urbana, he was on his way to Trinidad.

CHAPTER 7—TRINIDAD
Island Life

The social, friendly, honest man, Whate'er he be,
'Tis he fulfils great Nature's plan, And none but he.
– **Robert Burns**

Professor Doland and his two new graduates were met at the dock in Port-of-Spain by an army officer who asked, *"Which of you is Mr. Muir?"* Logan identified himself and was told to sit in front beside the driver. He was mildly curious about being singled out, but this was over-shadowed by the exhilaration of being on this interesting tropical island where everything was new to him.

Professor Doland and Ken Compton were dropped off in town, and Logan's curiosity increased as the driver headed easterly out of Port-of-Spain. Finally they came to a construction site where he was introduced to the army officer in charge. The officer wasted no time. He took Logan to a heap of stone and gravel, picked up a handful, and asked, *"Can we make concrete runways out of this?"*

Logan knew immediately why he was there. With his work at the Portland Cement Association, his numerous experiments had told him what the requirements were for concrete to withstand certain pressures and elements of nature. The knowledge gained while working four years as a menial beaker washer and concrete tester was valuable. Everyone on the site knew what to do; the only thing they needed to begin the runways was a "Yes".

Logan picked up a handful of the mixture, fingered it, and said, *"Yes,"* with confidence and little hesitation. The officer turned to the foreman of the crew and yelled, *"We'll make it out of concrete!"* The foreman turned to the next man in line, shouted the same, and immediately the entire area, which had been at a standstill waiting for a go-ahead, became a scene of intense activity.

It might have been Logan's first experience with a project of this magnitude that rested entirely on his judgment. It might have given his confidence a boost. He might have been awed by the responsibility involved. Whatever his thoughts, he never shared them. He did know he was now a graduate engineer with some experience and expertise of value.

The airfield was constructed at Cumuto about 25 miles east of Port-of-Spain on the Great Western Road. Logan oversaw the runway construction, working six days a week, 10 hours a day. Dump trucks carried the concrete to the proposed runway site where it was mixed and poured. At his suggestion the mixer was placed on a movable platform to facilitate loading and discharge. When the mixer operator was sick for a week, Logan filled in at his job. It was stripped-to-the-waist physical labor in the hot tropical sunshine, yet he had nothing but favorable comments about his life in Trinidad.

Logan and Ken found a boarding house in Port-of-Spain at 96 Maraval. It was a stately house with always-open louvered windows on each side, and a wide overhang to keep out the tropical rains which were heavier than any he had ever experienced. The rains were warm, and once over, the intense sun came out again.

The food at the boarding house was tropical fare. The only local produce safe to eat were those foods with skins to peel—bananas, papayas, mangoes. Fresh greens, such as lettuce, had to be washed in a solution of potassium permanganate, which left them with an unappetizing purple appearance. Fresh milk was not safe to drink. Instead, Logan ate without complaining, and even with happy anticipation, what the locals ate.

Such was not the case with two of the boarders at 96 Maraval. To call them "boors" would be complimentary. They often complained about the food, and, if they didn't like it, dumped it out the open window. The landlady couldn't get angry–she feared unknown consequences. Logan and Ken accepted this behavior at first, but one day it was–to put it simply–once too often. By previous mutual agreement, Logan and Ken confronted the boors and escorted them to the door. There was a scuffle, but it was the end of their disagreeable behavior and presence. The landlady was grateful to be rid of them. She had been doing her best for these "ugly Americans" with the resources at hand.

Ken's wife Beth eventually joined him in Trinidad. She procured secretarial work with the army headquarters, and she and Ken found a place of their own. It was through Beth that Logan met Erma Henke, the secretary to the Commanding General, Carib Area.

Erma and her husband Buddy had found a suitable house to rent at the edge of Port-of-Spain, where they would have space for two more people. Logan accepted their invitation to join them there, and two maids—Gertrude and her niece Loreen—would provide meals, laundry, and housekeeping services for their comfort. Gertrude made mushroom soup for them six days a week, and varied it with tomato soup once a week. The height of Logan's discontent at the time was in his usual response: *"What? Tomato soup again?"* He was enjoying Trinidad.

With completion of the airbase Logan's work often included air-trips to inspect and evaluate nearby sites. One such inspection trip took him on a flight to investigate the delta of the Orinoco River off the Venezuelan coast. They flew a short way out over the ocean and soon spotted one of Hitler's U-boats far below. As they watched intently, the U-boat silently slipped into the muddy waters, undoubtedly knowing they had been observed by the plane carrying the inspection team. The reality of war was never far from one's mind in that area.

In the office, Logan's civil engineering work continued. His hours were the same–ten hours a day, six days a week. On that seventh day he hiked around the island with the Henkes or Comptons or others, or went to Queen's Park Savannah to watch a local football game. The natives had a hard time understanding football, and were a little put off by the ambulance available at one end of the field.

The four house-mates got on well in their pleasant arrangement. By direction of the General, his car picked up Erma each morning and took her to work. The General's four stars on the license plate were hidden under the regulation cover, signifying that he was not in the vehicle.

One morning while the driver was waiting for Mrs. Henke, Logan was leaving for work. The driver struck up a conversation and asked where he was headed. When Logan responded, the driver said, "I'm going right by there...hop in and I'll drop you off before I drop off Mrs. Henke." This seemed like a decent arrangement: it was wartime, gas was a precious commodity, as was time, and Logan could get to work more easily.

Everyone knew the General's car with its covered license plate when he was not riding inside. When it entered the U-shaped driveway at

Logan's office building, heads appeared at the windows. It was a surprise to them to see Logan get out! And it wasn't just once–it was every day after that. Logan kept silent about the circumstances, but could sense the deference in the air as he went about his job. The General's working day at the office had not yet begun, but Erma knew the General would have approved.

Logan wrote to me about once a month during his Trinidad stay. The letters were colorful descriptions of events on that island which set it apart from life in the States. His enthusiastic comments were often accompanied by snapshots, but he said little about missing me. Before he left, I was not quite 18, and he said I was too young to make up my mind about a life partner. He was sure, he said, but wanted me to be sure also. *"Date other men,"* he said, *"and don't stay home."* So we parted in 1941 with no commitments.

Nevertheless, he sent gifts from time to time: Chanel No. 5 from Curacao, Netherlands West Indies; a sterling silver filigree bracelet from Trinidad. Accompanying the bracelet was a snapshot of a local woman selling oranges on the street. On her arms were many bracelets similar to mine, and on the back of the picture a note that these are often pure silver and the woman wears $250 to $300 worth which has accumulated over several generations.

Logan sent many snapshots which showed the local scenery and culture, and how it differed from the States. One picture showed a native squatting on his haunches in an open area. Beside him is a small fire on which he is heating his bit of lunch and in the near background is a brand new high-rise office building. The contrast was striking.

The local black people were often very poor, living in shacks that were cobbled together from any kind of scrap available, yet it was a surprise to hear them speak with very proper English accents.

Barber shops were portable, set up wherever the trade happened to be. The heat of the day was siesta time, and at mid-day a man spread his mat where he chose–frequently a shaded doorway–and curled up for a nap.

During business hours the main street of Port-of-Spain was jammed with bicycles, trams, autos, cars, and pedestrians. The big department stores–Stevens, Millers, Davidson & Todd–were busy, high-priced, and barn-like.

After work Logan and his house-mates sat on their cool porch, and were frequently serenaded by calypso singers. The charm of the calypso was in the talent of the singer as he looked at his audience and the setting, and skillfully wove them into impromptu musical rhymes.

The steel drum band originated in Trinidad but had no prominence before 1941. As the European war raged on, oil was imported in huge drums and the empty drums accumulated. The resourceful natives carefully cut these empty drums to graduated heights and used them to make the notes of the musical scales. The music had an ethereal quality and the distinctive tones became a steel band signature world-wide.

It was in Trinidad that Logan first learned about Angostura Bitters, a native product. During later years Logan perfected a tasty old-fashioned cocktail, with all the proper proportions of ingredients including, especially, the bitters. His old fashioneds were one cocktail this lady enjoyed on special occasions.

Much later, after Logan returned to the states, Gertrude was ill and needed costly medical treatment. Logan sent money to help pay for it, and Gertrude responded with this letter. Erma, of course, was "Madam".

2 Cascade Road
October 19, 1942

Dear Mr. Logan
Loreen and I so glad you ritten to us we meast you very much... I was sich after you gone...madam was very nice to me I went to the Doctor madam tould you what he told me I am much better I am not feling the pain again so I wonte [need] the money you sent me thank you very much Madam senting it back with my best thank that very kind of you I am glad your Mother find you got fat thank hair for saying so of me madam make cake every Sunday Mr. Henke tak two or three paces to work Mr. Gibson rite he is marrie so I hope you will soon get marrie to Madam have a little cat Mr. Henke don't like it so much so is a jock [joke] in the huse Mr. Harry came for a few days last mounth madam work in the graden got

sunburn if you see heir back it is brown it is hot these days
I hope you will like the Army and they will sent you to
Trinidad
Loreen joine with me

I remain Gertrude Philbert

On Sunday, December 1941, Logan and several friends were hiking around the island and heard the alarming Pearl Harbor news when they returned home. With the congressional declaration of war on Japan and Germany, the people of the United States were anxious to do whatever was necessary to win. Shortly after war was declared, this letter was in *Time Magazine's* "Letters to the Editor" section. The writer expressed the frustration, yet eagerness, of many U.S. citizens at that time:

> *...We're achingly eager to help, to know, to act and we have been for a long time...Every man and woman in the nation should be drafted at once for war work. Those of us who can't fight can learn to make airplanes. Those of us who can't make airplanes can darn the airplane makers' sox or cook their meals. Some of us can register those who are drafts. Some of us can answer telephones and lick stamps and run errands. Surely there is a place for everyone. March 9, 1942.*

By mid-1942 Logan's engineering work in Trinidad was essentially completed and he longed to get back to the U.S. to join the Navy. It took time, and cutting red tape, to be released from his duties there. Finally in the early fall he and Joe Kettle were permitted to leave. This time they flew across the water and rented a room in a posh Florida hotel. Their first request was for a couple of pitchers of milk to be sent to their rooms!

At that time telegrams were sent to convey news of great, immediate importance. His wire to me was brief. He was back in the states, he said, and *"...milk sure is good."* Reading between the lines I knew he would be in touch soon. However, Joe and Logan first had business at the Navy Recruiting Office in Chicago.

CHAPTER 8—UNCLE SAM NEEDS YOU
A Romance Develops

He serves me most, who serves his country best.
– Alexander Pope

Joe Kettle and Logan sat side by side in the recruiting office, awaiting physicals which, if passed, would permit immediate naval assignment. Joe passed his and was assigned to a U.S. Navy destroyer. Logan wore glasses, which made him ineligible for sea duty. However, the newly-formed Construction Battalions (familiarly called the Seabees) could accept him, but there was one hurdle uncovered by the physical exam. Logan did not have enough chest expansion. He asked the Navy doctor how he could overcome that.

"Go home and chop wood," the doctor said. Though the Muirs had no wood-burning stove and little use for chopped wood, he returned to Clarendon Hills and energetically chopped away. No word on what they did with the chopped wood. But he passed the physical and in November, 1942, was duly sworn into the Navy as an Assistant Civil Engineer with the rank of Ensign. Even without the official document that arrived later, he had no reservations about the seriousness of his pledge.

The
President of the United States of America
To all who shall see these presents, greetings
Know Ye, that reposing special Trust and Confidence in the Patriotism, Valor, Fidelity and Abilities of
LOGAN NAPIER MUIR, JR.,
I do appoint him Assistant Civil Engineer with the rank of Ensign in the Naval Reserve of the United States Navy to

*rank from the Twenty-First day of November 1942. He is
therefore carefully and diligently to discharge the duties of
such office by doing and performing all manner of things
thereunto belonging. And I do strictly charge and require
all Officers, Seamen and Marines under his Command to
be obedient to his orders. And he is to observe and follow
such orders and directions from time to time as he shall
receive from me, or the future President of The United
States of America or his Superior Officer set over him,
according to the Rules and Discipline of the Navy.
This Commission to continue in force during the pleasure
of the President of the United States for the time being.
Done at the City of Washington this Twenty-Fifth day of
November in the year of our Lord One Thousand Nine
Hundred and Forty-Two and of the Independence of the
United States of America the One Hundred and Sixty-
Seventh.*

*By the President:
Frank Knox
Secretary of the Navy*

At Marshall Field's department store in Chicago's Loop the new
ensign was outfitted with uniform requirements: dress blues, dress whites
for summer, khakis, shoes, boots, gloves, and other accoutrements, all
in preparation for the arrival of official active duty orders.

During the weeks before his orders arrived, he had time to think
about his future. These were sobering times, made more so when he
learned that his friend Joe Kettle had gone down with his destroyer in
the South Pacific. Logan was 28 and wanted very much to get married.
*"I want to arrange all of my affairs so you'll be taken care of if anything
happens to me in the war,"* he told me. He would have GI insurance,
of course, as did all service people, but it was not customary–and
perhaps not even permitted–to name a non-relative as beneficiary. But
he understood, also, the importance my family gave to education. Our
decision was to delay marriage until I graduated.

As the months ground on during my junior year, he found time
to come to Urbana, and occasionally I went to Clarendon Hills. In

Chicago he wooed me with an evening at the musical, "_Porgy and Bess_". He was an officer and a gentleman as he dazzled this lady with an evening dinner at the Blackstone Hotel in the Loop. Each evening must have cost at least five dollars.

But the best parts of our time together were the light-hearted long walks near his home with their collie, Tammy. We talked and dreamed and explored the almost unlimited possibilities in our future together. His mother was very kind, even though she thought of me as scrawny. Years later, Logan confided that she said to him, *"Don't you ever lay a hand on that little girl."* Long before I heard of this admonition I knew Logan would take good care of me.

Ensign Logan Muir and Ma – he wasn't sure
he would survive the war

When the active duty orders finally arrived, preparation time was short. His first duty was at the Board of Trade Building in Chicago where he reported to a medical officer for final approval. The man in front of him identified himself as Ensign Jensen. In that serious moment Logan could barely suppress his laughter at the rhyme in his handle. Ensign Jensen didn't think it was funny. Yet, in the ways of war and the world-wide expansion of the Navy's duties, their paths crossed later in unexpected ways.

Logan was ready to travel to Norfolk, Virginia, but knew nothing about Navy protocol. His train stopped in a land-locked town in Ohio where he got off to make a few minor purchases. The usual dark uniform in that midwest city was on a bell captain. A little old lady approached him with an urgent query: *"Can you tell me on which track the train for Chicago leaves?"*

Things became more complicated when enlisted men began saluting him. He struggled through it all as best he could and was glad to arrive in Norfolk where he could get answers for some of his questions.

At Camp Peary near Williamsburg, Virginia, he was attached to the 90th CB Battalion as part of Headquarters Company. The Seabees' song which was popular at the time, explains their mission:

> *We're the Seabees of the Navy;/ We can build and we can fight./We'll pave the road to victory,/ And guard it day and night./And we promise that we'll remember/ The seventh of December/ We're the Seabees of the Navy/ Bees of the Seven Seas!*

Some wags even boasted that the Marines landed on roads built by the Seabees. A slight exaggeration, perhaps, but the Seabees needed to be trained to fight, which is what a construction battalion or maintenance unit had to do if they were the early forces to land on enemy-held territory. So the Seabees were sent to the Marine base at Camp LeJeune, North Carolina, to train with Marine recruits.

It wasn't long before some of Logan's men came to him and said the Marines were stealing their gear. His Seabees were expected to be civil and honest, and certainly not thieves. Further, their impression was that the enemies were the Axis powers, not Americans in uniform. Logan complained to the officer in charge of the Marines and was given the equivalent of a brush-off. "*That's war,*" was the indifferent reply.

It's necessary to understand the Seabees' background to appreciate what followed. Seabees had been construction men in civilian life: tough, hardened, muscular, and worldly, and accustomed to solving problems in a practical way. Many of them were older than the Marine recruits. Logan essentially told his men he'd close his eyes the next time the stealing occurred if they handled it however they chose. The young marine recruits were naïve beside these experienced Seabees. Whatever ensued went un-reported, and un-noticed except perhaps for a few bloody noses. The stealing stopped.

Back in Norfolk at their own base Logan was asked by the Captain to round up all the misfits, parolees, and any unsavory characters that were arriving on base from time to time.

"Let's get rid of them", the Captain ordered. *"Add enough new recruits to the list to make a full complement for a CBMU* [Construction Battalion Maintenance Unit]."

Logan followed instructions to the letter. He needed to add only a handful of raw recruits to make the full complement. When he reported to the Captain, he was told,

> *Ensign Muir, after embarkation leave, you will take these men up to Providence, Rhode Island, and we'll ship them all out. You will be in charge.*

Logan once said he never volunteered in the Navy, and of course he never refused an assignment. He expected this unit composed of misfits might be a challenge.

After both Mr. And Mrs. C. had died, this letter from Logan was found among things my parents thought worth keeping.

> *19 August 1943*
> *Dear Mr. And Mrs. C,*
> *I should have written you folks a long time ago, but I hope in the meantime Ruthie has been passing on some of the news and my best regards to you. I was disappointed that I could not visit you in Urbana the last time I was home but the furlough was so short I thought I ought to spend all of it with Ma and Pa. After all we don't all of us get home safely from a war.*
> *The weather there in Urbana should start getting cooler now as late August and the autumn approaches. I always enjoyed the fall months down there more than any of the others… Today was a wonderfully cool but sunny day—a real joy to be alive and breathing, but it did make me homesick for Urbana.*
> *I want to thank you also for letting Ruthie come in and stay with me and the folks during my stay at home. I have never known a girl that is as good-natured and easy to get along with as Ruthie and there is none I would rather be*

*with. She is a lovely and wonderful little girl and I know
the credit belongs to both of you for that, too. She is the
kind of 'well-bred' that begins in the home. I am sure it is
no secret to you that I intend to marry her should this war
spare me and I will try to continue to furnish a home for
her as she has known up to now. I am going to send her a
ring for her birthday, something to help her to remember
me and I hope you will understand that it is with the
sincerest motives..."*

On the train ride north from Virginia one of Muir's men came to him with the suspicion that they were all being shipped out because they were problems. Logan replied immediately: *"I would not have hand-picked you to go out with me if I had thought you were problems."* This was true, of course, but hardly in the way the recruit thought. Yet it calmed the unrest on board.

But problems did surface. As he walked through the train, Ensign Muir detected the distinct smell of liquor. He called in his Chief and said, *"... find out who has the liquor and see that you dispose of it."* The affable Chief agreed to do his best. The liquor seemed to disappear for a time, but when it appeared again, the Chief was called in, and again he assured Ensign Muir that he would get to the bottom of it..."*And let me know who is supplying it,"* Muir added.

After several such encounters, it turned out that the Chief himself was putting liquor into the water dispenser at the end of the car. Suitable reprimands were given and Muir gained new insight into the kinds of recruits in his charge.

At Providence the contingent waited to be shipped out. One of his new recruits came to him with an urgent plea: *"Ensign Muir, I absolutely have to have leave so I can get married."*

There was time enough during the delay, but there was another problem. *"You know the rules—you're all confined to base waiting for a ship. What's so urgent? Why now?"* Muir probed.

*"I got my girl in a family way, and I've got to take care
of her. If I could just marry her, her family won't hold it
against her."*

Muir was not easily persuaded, yet recognized a sincerity about this man he barely knew. Finally he said, *"I'll see what I can do."*

The next time the Captain in charge was given a sheaf of papers to sign, buried inside was one authorizing leave for the new recruit.

"You know what this means, don't you?" Muir reminded the man as he handed him the authorization. *"If the Captain finds out about this we'll both be in trouble."* The man assured him he'd return within the time limit. He was true to his word and his gratitude made him one of Muir's most loyal men.

Logan had one more personal detail to tend to before shipping out. He picked out a diamond ring and mailed it to me from Providence. I asked Mr. C. to put it on my finger, and as he did, he said, *"This is surely providential..."*

CHAPTER 9—ANCHORS AWEIGH
A Friendly Face on Shore

Seas roll to waft me, suns to light me rise;
My footstool earth, my canopy the skies
– Alexander Pope

On 12 September 1943 a troop ship named the *Santa Monica* left Providence, Rhode Island, for ports unknown to all but the ship's Captain. Logan was attached to the 7th Garrison Detachment on board. They would learn their destination after they were underway. Total blackout was enforced en route, the ship was crowded, and the officers' quarters below were stuffy.

Ever the man with practical solutions, Logan and a fellow-officer decided to sleep topside where they secured their hammocks out over the water. For several nights they enjoyed identifying stellar constellations made incredibly brilliant against the blacked-out sky. They watched as the North Star gradually became lower in the northern horizon, and felt the breezes become warmer as the ship sailed into equatorial waters. When the waves and swells of the ocean slapped against the ship their hammocks swayed in harmony. Paradise itself!

The Captain eventually learned of their precarious solution and ordered them to spend their remaining nights safely below deck in their cabins.

As the *Santa Monica* made its way through the locks of the Panama Canal and toward the Pacific Ocean, Logan eagerly scanned the ship's passage and the area on both sides of the locks. As he did so he looked up to see Ensign Jensen waving at him from land. They shouted brief surprised pleasantries, but hardly expected to see each other again. After all, there was a war on and the South Pacific was a vast area.

At the crossing of the equator, all hands on board who were crossing for the first time were initiated as Shellbacks into the "Solemn Mysteries of the Ancient Order of the Deep". The initiation details remain a mystery. I was told only that they were appropriate and thorough.

The ship took a southwesterly heading, zigzagging and varying its speed so as to confuse the enemy and avoid becoming a target. Finally it arrived at Pago Pago, American Samoa, where the friendly face waiting on the dock was, of course, Ensign Jensen! Both officers were then attached to CBMU 506 where they shared quarters until April, 1944.

Overseas duty often meant sleeping in tents. However, the previous Seabee residents [construction men in civilian life] had used their spare time to build permanent quarters for themselves. When their military orders sent them on to other areas, they left behind well-built accommodations for the next arriving Seabees.

Eleven officers made up the complement of CBMU 506. Each had a specialized function in the Unit's operation. They honed their battle skills and remained in a state of readiness as they waited for posting to any forward area. That was the way of war: back-up support, waiting, constant preparation, waiting, and always ready for the next assignment.

Logan's assignment on Samoa was Transportation Officer. One of his responsibilities was overseeing the regularly scheduled Navy bus that drove around the island transporting men to their duty stations. On one such oversight inspection tour he noticed that the bus passed a local Samoan who was one of the Samoan military. They all wore the lava lava instead of khakis, but were very much a part of the island's defenses. They knew every detail about the island: where boats could safely dock; where special defenses were needed; where to take proper shelter; where the natives lived. Logan instructed his driver to back up and pick up the Samoan. Back at his desk he devised plans and bulletins to include them in the local bus service in the future.

It might have been the informality of the lava lava that caused some of the servicemen to make fun of the natives and call them "gooks". Even the commander of the base had a bias against them, and when he heard about Logan's directives, explanations were in order. *"How strange,"* Logan said, *"that someone on our side in the war was not accepted as an equal partner."* Logan finally prevailed but not without using his logic and powers of persuasion to convince his commanding officer that they should be included in the bus service.

"Loose lips sink ships," was a common admonition to every U.S. citizen during the war. All mail from servicemen was censored. The officers' mail was censored by superior officers, and Logan, too, censored

mail. It was well-known that some letters arrived in the U.S. with words blacked out. Logan was meticulous about following "Navy regs". His letters were mostly descriptions of island life, but included nothing of a military nature—no geographic names, no locale described in a recognizable manner, and no mention or even hint of military operations or objectives. Never were any of his words or phrases blacked out.

Back in Illinois one day Ma and Pa read a report in the *Chicago Daily News* by a journalist who had been to Samoa and was shown around the island by the Transportation Officer stationed there. The reporter was discreet and didn't name the officer, but mentioned that he was from Clarendon Hills. Ma and Pa knew immediately, from descriptions, that that officer was Logan. Certainly the journalist meant no harm, but for the Muirs it was a missing puzzle piece and emphasized how "loose lips", though innocent themselves, can provide valuable information. I need hardly add that this newly discovered intelligence never went past the confines of the Muir household.

Logan did write to me about a beautiful young native girl who came to the officer's club. She had been a stand-in for Dorothy Lamour during her tropical "Road" films with Bing Crosby and Bob Hope. Logan also sent me a grass skirt and an assortment of native necklaces–some were made from sea shells, some from native seeds. All were intricately strung together and to this day, their clever skill remains a mystery to me. The necklaces were definitely not the work of "gooks".

Emergencies, readiness and teamwork exercises, or forward assignments required constant attention, but after fulfilling duty assignments on Samoa there was usually some free time. He wrote to me as often as possible, and numbered his letters so they could be put in proper order when received, though they seldom arrived in order. It was a long-distance courtship. Too many men got a "Dear John" letter from a sweetheart or fiancée who broke off her engagement when she found someone else at home that she liked better. The old adage, "absence makes the heart grow fonder...", sometimes had tacked on at the end, "...for someone else." Logan wanted to make sure that didn't happen to us.

To fill in the reader on the life of Logan's fiancée, it is necessary to provide a few details. I finished my senior year at Illinois in 1944 with a major in nutrition and dietetics. The usual next step would be a year's dietetic internship in a hospital. I was offered several plum choices: Walter Reed Hospital near Washington D.C., Massachusetts General in Boston, or Barnes in St. Louis. There would be no salary, but all expenses of uniforms, room and board were provided. However, for me there was one stumbling block: it was to be a full calendar year, during which the apprentice dietitian could not marry.

It was a wrenching decision. The "could not marry" directive weighed heavily on my mind. Logan was almost 30 and we wanted very much to get married when Navy orders would return him to the States. When I wrote him that I felt like throwing the whole thing overboard (meaning, of course, the dietetics pre-training), he responded with a bit of doggerel. Here is part of his light-hearted response to my agony.

PRESENTING A POEM
entitled
THROW THE WHOLE THING OVERBOARD
by
Ens. L.N. Muir, Poet Laureate, USNR

(Title courtesy of Miss Ruth Claussen whose
immortal words they are.)

Editor's note: Occasionally there appears on the Horizon
of Letters one who ranks with such poetic greats as Alfred
Lord Tennyson, Percy Bysshy (or sumpin') Shelley, John
Milton, Sears Roebuck, Ladies Underwear, Children's
Shoes, Leather Goods, Third Floor, All out!!! Well, anyhow,
the author aint one of them. In fact, his rhymes are the
most painful ever penned by a literary aspirant. In fact,
the author ought to be penned! Well, folks, somebody put a
nickel in so we gotta listen to it – I give you – and you can
keep it – Throw the Whole Thing Overboard:

I

"Throw the WHOLE THING overboard,"/ Bellowed

Captain to the crew /As they took apart the anchor/Which, as everybody knew/When you come into a port/Is not the thing to do./For an anchor that's in pieces/Or even cut in two/Won't keep a ship from driftin'/And so I'm telling you,/ Throw the WHOLE THING overboard!

II

The boy stood on the burning deck/His pants were all aflame/His ship was burning stem to stern/The lad was not to blame./Then looking up with pleading eyes/"What shall I do?"/ His thin voice cries/"My ship's afire/ My pants aflame/Down in the hold/ It is the same/The whole darned thing Has caught afire/What shall I do Almighty Sire?"/A voice from out the cloudy sky/Did answer with a heavy sigh,/"Throw the whole thing overboard."

[Several more verses followed]
FINIS (Aint you glad?)

There were not a lot of reasons for humor during the war, and some might read his poetry and say he'd been "out there" too long. But Logan's light-hearted approach scored a home-run, so to speak. I saw no attempt in his words to persuade me either to take—or not to take--the year's internship. His rhyming words touched my funny bone. Later in life he did occasionally say that he married me because I laughed at his jokes.

But this was war-time. Divergent thoughts raced through my mind. I thought of my sister and sister-in-law, each with a toddler to care for at home. I thought of my other sister who had just joined the Army as a hospital dietitian. I thought of the year as an intern in the hospital when I couldn't marry. I thought of the war, which everyone hoped would soon be over. I thought of Logan's loyalty to the U.S. Navy.

For me, I wanted to help end the war. *"Free a man for active duty"* was on the military recruitment ads aimed at single women. I could not envision how my year as an intern in a hospital would help end the war sooner. My decision, then, was to forego the internship. Instead of becoming a dietitian, I joined the U.S. Navy WAVES (Women Accepted for Volunteer Emergency Service). That part was relatively

57

easy compared with one of the last meetings with my advisor at the University. I had the humiliating feeling that Professor E. Evelyn Smith would never forgive me.

It was a good decision in some ways. Certainly it was the patriotic thing to do; it also helped me understand, throughout later years, Logan's dedicated Navy service. But it also presented a drawback which I had not anticipated until I was in Navy boot camp later.

As I neared graduation in May, 1944, Logan was still on Samoa when he received orders to the forward island of Tarawa. Six months earlier, in November, 1943, that beleaguered island had been the scene of one of World War II's bloodiest Pacific battles. With the island finally secured, the Seabees would move in and provide construction needed to hold it—air fields, roads, accommodations. Everyone knew this forward area might still be subjected to recurring attacks by the Japanese. Logan acknowledged, if asked, that he accepted without complaint any assignment the Navy gave him, and Tarawa was no exception.

Before the orders to Tarawa could be carried out, however, new orders arrived telling him to join the 20th Seabee Battalion on the island of Banika in the Russell Islands, a part of the Guadalcanal group. These orders he accepted also without wavering or complaint.

The 20th Seabees had been overseas for some time and the men were expecting to be sent home soon for much-needed rest and recreation (R&R). Not everyone was happy to see new men arrive—it could mean their return to the States was delayed. However, Logan's new tent-mate was Lt. Arneth Christensen. Arneth was not one to get over-wrought about events over which he had no control. The two maintained a life-long friendship.

My eight weeks of Navy boot camp training began in late September. The first weeks were intense indoctrination into the Navy's protocol and methods. Little by little I was beginning to understand Logan's Navy life. A letter dated September 30, 1944, to my parents described my early impressions.

> *Dearest Mom and Dad,*
> *I'm going to write now because it's hard telling when I'll*
> *be so busy I can't…if you don't hear from me just know*
> *I'm studying, drilling, etc…[Navy life] is… exacting…*

each day it becomes easier [for me] *to be exacting. Our*
rooms always look neat as anything... yesterday Filene's
of Boston measured us for uniforms and they are the
most comfortable and well-made suits I've ever had...I
bought over $100. worth of suits, raincoat, gloves, hose,
and shirts... all paid for by the Navy!... prices are rather
high...suits are $25., the raincoat which has a removable
lining and serves also as a winter overcoat is about $35...
nice looking too!... Most of the things we learn are classed
as "restricted" information so I can't tell you too much
about it... they also take good care of us. The exercises,
drill, and eight hours' sleep are good for us... physically
as well as for disciplinary reasons... Haven't heard from
Logan for nearly two weeks. Wonder where he is now...

I could not know that, at about that same time, the 20th Naval Construction Battalion was on a ship sailing home under the Golden Gate Bridge in California. Their destination would be the Construction Battalions' Camp Parks, adjacent to the Navy's Camp Shoemaker near Pleasanton. All of the men would be given leave before reporting back there for new assignments. Leave time back in the 48 states was the ultimate R&R (rest and recreation). It meant time at home with family and friends, and for Logan it included a visit to Northampton, Mass. to see me. We had hoped to be married upon his return. Now I had created a new dilemma: not only could I not get married, but during the first four weeks, apprentice seamen in the WAVES were restricted to town.

Logan and I solved it the way we usually approached problems. He came to Northampton, we walked around that beautiful town full of large homes set in huge lawns, made our way down to the nearby Connecticut River, marveled at the brilliant show put on by the autumn leaves, enjoyed an occasional restaurant meal together, and when he reported back to Camp Parks, the long- distance courtship/romance continued with letters and weekly phone calls. We still had no idea what the Navy had in mind for my future. But the Navy did.

They assigned me to eight weeks of further training in Northampton as a Communications Officer. Assignment beyond that was unknown. It was generally understood, however, that upon completion, most ComSchool WAVES were sent to the Washington, D.C. area. A handful went to other locations—New Orleans or Seattle or San Francisco. WAVES could request a location, but nothing was guaranteed. My request was for San Francisco which would be as close to Camp Parks as I could get. One of Logan's letters ended with *"…I can't live without you…"* We both hoped the Navy would be kind.

CHAPTER 10—NAVY LIFE TO CIVILIAN LIFE
A Solemn Day

Till a' the seas gang dry, my dear,
And the rocks melt wi' the sun!
And I will luve thee still, my dear,
While the sands o' life shall run.
– **Robbie Burns**

Finally in late January, after what seemed an unnecessarily long wait, the orders began to come through for the ComSchool WAVES. Whoops and hollers and excitement filled the dorm halls.

Those sent to New Orleans were excited about the colorful Mardi Gras about to begin; those heading for Washington, D. C. were enthusiastic about becoming involved in the hub of war activities; those going to San Francisco talked endlessly about the charm of that beautiful west coast city ready to fulfill the dreams of anyone longing to go there. To my happy relief, I was included in that last group.

Now at last Logan and I could be married. It was seven and a half years since we met at the dinner table. Our engagement had been only a fraction of that, and all of it with long distance letters and phone calls. I sent him my last long-distance message, a telegram which said simply, *"I can't live without you either will arrive February 4th"*.

In contrast to the simple message in the telegram, the subsequent activities bordered on pandemonium. There were medical exams, clothing purchases, family to inform, train reservations to coordinate, duty assignments to firm up and verify, and such mundane tasks as dry-cleaning, laundry, and packing my gear.

At Camp Parks in California Logan was involved in a similar flurry of activity. Hotel arrangements, shopping, a doctor's appointment and other necessary tasks filled his off duty hours. He arranged with Arneth and Frances Christensen to be best man and matron of honor. As became evident later, one thing he could not control was the Navy.

My cross country train trip to San Francisco took me through Chicago where my family gathered to give me a proper send-off. Mr. C. couldn't perform the ceremony, but his letter to us was full of his usual far-sighted wisdom and encouragement. He ended it, as he always did with family letters: Pi Alpha and Mu Alpha, the Greek letters for Pa and Ma:

February 1, 1945

Dear Ruthie and Logan:

This is your "D Day". You "have arrived", and are ready to embark again. That is real Navy life. Your wishes and plans have materialized. You have come to a focal point in your lives, where you can rejoice in each other's success and attainment thus far. You no doubt will glory <u>above all</u> in the gracious Providence of God who has spared your lives and led you on, all the way to your present stage of progress, which happily is also a state of exalted felicity.

…your day of arrival is also a day of embarkation, and that too in a special sense of the word. You are ready and probably anxious to embark on the sea of matrimony. While on the one hand you will sail under the "Stars and Stripes," on another and special sense you will sail under the leadership of the Captain of your life and salvation whom we salute with you in the beautiful words of the poem and hymn:

Jesus, Savior pilot me/Over life's tempestuous sea. / Unknown waves before me roll /Hiding rock and treacherous shoal./Chart and compass come from Thee,/ Fear not, I will pilot Thee.

You will very often sail under sealed orders, and may not

*know the destination and plan of your course. But you
will feel secure and safe, because of your faith and devotion
to your Captain... While on your voyage to the heavenly
goal you can always enjoy the harbor and safe retreat in
the lovely home you are now establishing and for this we
extend to you our heartiest congratulations. With fervent
prayers, fond hopes and best wishes. God bless you.*

Your Pi Alpha & Mu Alpha (alias) Mr. And Mrs. C.

Most passengers on the west-bound train from Chicago would be
taking the ferry from the Oakland Mole to San Francisco. But before
that final destination the train stopped briefly at Oakland's 16th Street
station where a few of us disembarked. The huge station was almost
empty, and I waited alone for Logan to arrive.

He finally appeared with the news that he was on duty as Officer of
the Day until 8:00 AM. It would not be the only time the Navy took
precedence over personal plans, but my Navy training made it easy to
understand. And of course, I could remind him for the rest of his life
how he kept me waiting at the station!

On that day––a Sunday––all the hospitality of the Christensens
was at our disposal. By Monday I knew well their eagerness to make our
wedding day memorable. Frances opened her closet door and consulted
me about what she should wear. I selected her navy blue suit which was
in harmony with the other three navy blue suits in the wedding party.
We stopped in town for a few purchases before having a celebratory
lunch together.

However, another unexpected hurdle arose: Monday is a day off
for many ministers. After unsuccessful attempts at several churches, we
found Rev. Frank Toothaker in his office at the First Methodist Church
in Oakland. He was used to performing wedding ceremonies for service
people, and probably wondered each time whether this was a spur of the
moment decision by the couple. More importantly, would it last.

He took us into his office where he spoke to us for more than an
hour about the seriousness of the vows we were about to take. The
ceremony itself was simple, and short. We four stood in front of the
minister in the huge sanctuary, all concentrating on the meaning and
solemnity of the vows with a minimum of distraction.

After the ceremony Arneth and Frances drove us across the Bay Bridge to San Francisco. There we went to the Top of the Mark Hopkins Hotel—the best place in the city with a 180 degree view of the city's Golden Gate Bridge, the ships, the islands, the waters and the Bay Bridge. One could almost walk across the bay–a distance of more than five miles–by going from ship to ship at anchor. For many servicemen that view from the hotel was their last look at the U.S. before heading out to unknown places.

Suddenly Logan said, *"Now what's yours is mine and what's mine's my own!"* For a moment I struggled with the idea that my vows had been a mistake. But logic returned and I realized that this was only his levity to ease the tension of a serious and solemn day.

Service uniforms were seen everywhere in the Bay area, and a uniformed person was given the red carpet treatment. The Hotel Leamington in Oakland provided an evening buffet "on the house" for anyone in uniform. However, because of the tremendous demand for rooms and the transient nature of clientele at that time, the hotel imposed a 3-day limit on registered guests.

The first day of our three-day honeymoon was spent exploring the University of California campus in Berkeley. It was green and lush that February, with lovely places to walk. It might have been between semesters because few people seemed to be there. Later that week we had our first separation when Logan returned to Camp Parks and I moved temporarily to the YWCA in San Francisco. It was close to my new duty station in the Federal Building.

Finally, after searching the crowded Bay Area, we found a place to live, and, after several weeks there during which we settled in and I reported for duty, Logan described our new "home" in a letter to my parents:

> *Dear Mr. & Mrs. C.*
> *This is really my first letter to a new set of parents, yet*
> *it's not so new because of the many years I lived in your*
> *home and enjoyed your friendship...being in the Navy*
> *together doesn't exactly amount to being together in the*
> *Navy. Yesterday I was required to remain at Camp Parks*
> *all day and last night so Ruthie came out here to keep me*
> *company. She arrived Saturday night and the WAVES*

*here…were kind enough to give her a room and a nice bed
to sleep in. Sunday morning she met me at the Officers'
Club for breakfast and we spent all day Sunday together.*

*Sunday night, however, she had to go back to our Oakland
headquarters so she could get to work in time this
morning. I had to stay out at Camp, so you see what I
mean.*

*Did she tell you about our place to live in Oakland? We
have a very fine big room with private bath, telephone,
and radio in a really beautiful home. It is in a very lovely
neighborhood, too, but oh boy, we're paying for all that!
Even though it is quite expensive, we are happy to have a
wholesome place to live. It is convenient, too, being only
a block from the train that takes Ruthie over to her job in
San Francisco and only two blocks from the highway to
Camp Parks…*

*The fruit trees are all in bloom… as well as numerous
shrubs and flowers and it's hard to realize that you folks
are still having winter…[will] write to everyone as soon
as we are a little more settled—it's a bit hectic just now
because of Ruthie's new job and our new living quarters…
hope to see you all before too long. Love, Logan*

The hectic part of those early days of our marriage was my schedule.
The Navy assigned me to rotating hours each week—two days of duty
from 7 a.m. to 3 p.m., followed by 24 hours off; then two days of duty
from 3 p.m. to 11 p.m., followed by 24 hours off; then two days of duty
from 11 p.m. to 7 a.m., followed by 24 hours off. After that the entire
week's schedule started over again. It was difficult even for younger
people to function with those constant 'round the clock changes in
hours.

Mix in with my schedule was Logan's schedule, which regularly
meant Officer-of-the-Day duty, when he was on call at Camp Parks
for 24 hours. The wonder is that we were able to see each other at all.

Sometimes, I would be going out the front door just as he was arriving home.

There were perks, however. Occasionally Logan would be driven to San Francisco on Navy business. At that time we arranged to have lunch together at Fisherman's Wharf. By that time he was a staff officer Lieutenant in the Civil Engineer Corps, and I was a line officer Ensign. Navy regs stipulate that in event of an emergency and regardless of rank, a line officer would have command over a staff officer. I occasionally reminded him of that technicality and offered to create an emergency so I could take over.

From time to time I went to Camp Parks during my time off. The WAVES stationed there were most hospitable and always found comfortable accommodations for me. We ate in the officer's mess where the food was excellent, and managed to spend a few hours on base together. But this was war time, and everyone made sacrifices. If ours was a sacrifice, it was minor.

The orange-colored Key System commuter trains crossed the Bay Bridge on the lower deck, where half the width was for the trains and half for trucks. The upper deck was two-directional auto traffic, with a 50-cent toll each way. As I rode from Oakland to my duty station at the Federal Building, the big train windows afforded a magnificent view of the Bay. For someone from the flat lands of Illinois this was a magical place, with the bridges and hills and towns beckoning to be explored.

In 1945 San Francisco was clearly a Navy town with dress blue uniforms everywhere. Civilians appeared in their Sunday best: men in suits and hats, women with hats, gloves and heels. The Emporium, Gumps, and the City of Paris offered unique quality merchandise. Cable cars clanged up and down the hills, and at the turn-table everyone helped push the cars around before they climbed aboard for the next cable-car trip. It was pure excitement to take it all in.

> *And joyful nations join in leagues of peace.*
> **– Alexander Pope**

By April of 1945 San Francisco hosted an international body of impressive dignitaries to work on the emerging United Nations charter. I was among a number of Navy WAVES on teletypes to Washington, D.C. to transmit messages to and from our own elected and appointed officials. By today's standards, news traveled slowly, and one day when I rode the elevator to my duty station someone announced that our President was dead.

It was clear from recent photographs that President Roosevelt had aged during his terms in office, but few people expected his death. The country was shocked at its loss and thrown into a period of mourning, coupled with a new uncertainty about the future.

The European war was not yet over, though there were signs of Germany's weakening. The war in the Pacific was a different story: it could go on much longer. The country had expected that Roosevelt would see the global war to its successful conclusion. And who was this Harry Truman, the Vice-President who would now become President? Roosevelt selected him as his running mate only a few months before, and people hoped he would be up to the responsibilities that went with the new title thrust upon him.

Harry Truman hoped so, too. He became known as a man with a moral integrity who had a sign on his desk, *"The buck stops here"*. He was faced with enormous decisions, one of which was the atomic bomb. Few people knew the complete story of the atomic bomb—how it was developed, where it could be used, what were its effects.

I learned years later that my brother, a physical chemist with a PhD degree from Illinois, was called to New York during that period, spent about 6 months developing answers to pertinent questions related to his field of expertise, and returned to his regular job with the Texas Company [Texaco], all without knowing how his replies fit into a larger picture. He is certain, in retrospect, that the questions pertained to the bomb.

On a related note, Dana, Logan's boyhood friend from Clarendon Hills, met us for lunch in San Francisco one day. He was in an officer's uniform and on his way to the South Pacific. Shortly afterward the bomb was dropped on Hiroshima. Years later Logan said he felt certain Dana was going there because of some activity related to the atomic bomb.

Much has been said and written about the morality of the use of the bomb. After-the-fact arguments have been heated. I knew only that the American casualties in the war were mounting, the Japanese enemy was tenacious in its determination to win, and securing the vast Pacific area island by island had already been a series of long bloody battles. When the war came to an abrupt end in late summer there was rejoicing in the streets of San Francisco after all the pent-up emotions and determination that had ruled everyone's life for so long.

During the summer of 1945 our housing had changed several times from that first expensive master bedroom in Oakland, to shared quarters near Oakland's Lake Merritt, to a re-modeled chicken coop in Hayward, which provided two rooms and a private bath. The kitchen was newly equipped with small appliances and a few dishes. A fenced yard was adjacent to our "chicken coop", where the owner kept a large dog, which barked loudly as dogs will do when disturbed. But we were ecstatic as we walked back and forth between two small rooms that were entirely ours. We decided we were coming up in the world.

By war's end the 20th Seabee Battalion had returned to the South Pacific, Logan was assistant public works officer at Camp Parks, and we were expecting our first child. Another housing "promotion" occurred when an apartment vacancy appeared in Komandorski Village at Camp Parks. Now we had a proper kitchen, a living room and a bedroom. Posh accommodations, indeed!

With the end of the war, Camp Parks became a discharge center for Construction Battalions returning from assignments in the Pacific area. The base had to prepare for the big influx of men expected. One of Logan's jobs as assistant public works officer was to provide sleeping quarters for returning servicemen. He put out an urgent request for mattresses from any base that could spare them.

Finally a box-car load of mattresses was delivered on the railroad siding. It was stuffed full of mattresses packed in so tightly they had to be pried out of the boxcar. Good news! Now the returning men would have something to sleep on. But it was a little like the sorcerer's apprentice. Another boxcar full of mattresses arrived. And another. And another. They had to unload them quickly or were charged per diem for delay. In a frenzy of activity his men found places for them, but officers later assigned to Camp Parks might have been surprised where they found mattresses.

By November, 1945, Logan, too, was scheduled to be separated from the Navy and we would have to give up our base housing at Komandorski Village. This was also the time frame when our first child was due. We had 30 days to vacate the apartment. We faced the uncertainties in a sensible way—we went to a movie at the base movie theater on December 4.

The next morning we knew the birth was imminent. The Navy had a saying at that time: *"You have to be there for the laying of the keel, but not for the launching of the ship."* After making suitable arrangements for my welfare Logan went to his office as usual. Perhaps it was not quite "as usual" because that morning the ship was launched, so to speak, and he became a father for the first time.

Events tumbled forward one on top of the other: a new son; return to civilian life; Christmas. The Navy was stringent in its rules: thirty days to vacate the apartment at Komandorski Village. We needed a place to live. Logan also needed to earn a living.

He solved part of the problem by buying a used car from a discharged serviceman flying home to the east. With a car he could bring his new son and me home from the hospital, and then address both the housing and employment problems.

He had saved a bit of money since college days, and with that in mind we started a search for housing for our growing family. Not knowing yet where future employment might be, we looked primarily in the East Bay area.

After time spent in a converted chicken coop, and later in a small apartment, we liked what we saw in a subdivision called San Lorenzo Village. The house we could afford had two bedrooms, a combination living-dining area, and a kitchen with a built-in breakfast nook. Luxury indeed! It was a newly-built tract house with no kitchen appliances, but was on a nice-sized lot where we could have a small garden. Between us and the Bay to the west was a stretch of open land, usually planted to sugar beets. The price was about $6500. On the loan application to buy one of those houses, Logan left a blank for the name of his employer—he had none. *"Come back when you have a job,"* he was told.

His logic immediately told him that the developer who built the houses would need a civil engineer, so within a day he applied at the David D. Bohannon Organization headquartered in San Mateo. He was hired on the spot as crew chief of a survey party, and he could now settle his family into a home. Solutions were beginning to fall into place. He expected, of course, that he would soon prove his worth and be promoted to civil engineer. If not, he was confident that the post-war economy would provide other opportunities.

Logan crossed the San Mateo bridge each day in a car-pool with several other employees of the Bohannon Organization. They rotated driving to allow their wives at home the use of their family cars once or twice a week.

The owner of the Bohannon Organization was a true gentleman. One morning at work Logan saw David D. Bohannon arrive in the parking lot and tip his hat to the cleaning woman who was just leaving. Logan always had an appreciative regard for working people, and this gesture from the owner of the business left a lasting impression on him.

Work was begun on the Hillsdale Shopping Center and the Woodside development. At work he gave his job his usual enthusiasm. He and his crew hacked their way through the thick brush and laid out survey lines. Someone casually warned him about poison oak, but coming from Illinois he knew only about poison ivy, and Logan had no fear. He wiped the sweat from his forehead again and again and continued his work. At home he unlaced his boots to take them off. These simple acts spread the oils from the poison oak plant further. Within a few days he had red itching sores over his face, his hands, his arms, his legs––a severe case of poison oak, caused by hacking through the brush. It finally became necessary to take a couple of weeks off.

Manufacturers had not yet re-tooled their equipment from war goods to household goods and it was impossible at that time to buy a new washing machine. Automatic washers were still on the drawing boards. Instead, I took all of our laundry to the nearest laundromat in San Leandro, which had the usual wringer-type washers and rinsing tubs. There his clothing was double-washed in the strongest soap on the market—yellow Fels Naphtha bar soap, shaved thin—in an attempt to get rid of all traces of the poison oak oils.

As for Logan, his face and arms swelled and he was almost unrecognizable from the distortion. He couldn't bend his elbows and had to be fed. The poison oak was deeply imbedded in his body and the itching and burning continued for almost a year. Gradually, after extreme vigilance and meticulous laundering those symptoms waned, but long before that, he returned to work and was promoted from survey chief to civil engineer. His dread of poison oak continued all of his life and affected our occasional housing decisions along the way.

When the war ended, the military had a huge quantity of surplus materiel for disposal. Double-decker beds, tents, dark green wool army blankets, vehicles, and many other military items were available to the public at reasonable prices. Mr. Cuykendall, Logan's superior, purchased a work vehicle at a bargain price and assigned it to Logan for his use on the job. It was armored and unwieldy, and much wider than a car. Logan hated using it on city streets because it was awkward and clumsy. It was one factor that played a part in his decision to leave the Bohannon Organization.

By the end of 1949 he had passed the registration exam for California Professional Engineer. With that new license he went to Sacramento to be interviewed for a job opening in the Division of Beaches and Parks. The interview was successful, and effective January 1, 1950, Logan began work there as a Professional Engineer.

By 1949 we had two small boys

CHAPTER 11—THE DIVISION OF BEACHES AND PARKS
Happy Days

Bliss was it in that dawn to be alive,
But to be young was very heaven!
– **William Wordsworth**

Logan was headquartered in Sacramento where he worked on development plans for newly acquired property for state parks and beaches. His job often took him to remote areas of the state to inspect and develop feasibility studies for possible access and public use. Informally, the Division was referred to as the "division of bushes and peaks", with good reason. Usually the property had a unique feature – a beach, redwood forest, or desert.

The lands involved had either been purchased by the state or, as was often the case, bequeathed to the state by a wealthy landowner who wanted them preserved for all time for public use. His work often took him to some of the most beautiful and remote undeveloped areas of the state. At such times he was given the use of a state vehicle.

By this time we had two young sons. Both were pre-schoolers and whenever practical and convenient Logan used our family car, instead of a state vehicle, and took us along. In this way we were able to enjoy the wilderness of the yet-to-be Jedediah Smith Redwoods State Park, the Prairie Creek Redwoods State Park, both in the far north, and many undeveloped parks throughout the state all the way down to the future Anza-Borrego Desert State Park in the far south. Logan's job always took precedence over family considerations, but just being along on these excursions gave the rest of us a chance to appreciate, even to this day, the beauty of the wilderness areas.

One evening Logan came home and told me of a new surveyor he had interviewed for a job. *"His name is Tim Train,"* Logan said, *"and I had the urge to ask him if he'd ever been out on a little toot."* He didn't know Tim well enough for that kind of levity, nor could he foresee that he and Tim might have a professional future together which did not involve the Division of Beaches and Parks.

As a newly-registered professional engineer in California, Logan took steps to join the Sacramento chapter of the California Society of Professional Engineers (C.S.P.E.). He was eager to keep up with the latest P.E. events and activities. At the first dinner meeting, he and other new P.E.s were introduced, and then asked to clear the dinner tables. He was sure that he had not come to the meeting to clear tables. He decided not to go back to further meetings since little of a professional nature was accomplished. When he did go back some time later, circumstances were different.

Tau Beta Pi is the National Engineering Society which recognizes high academic achievement in engineering studies. It had been nearly eleven years since Logan missed his graduation ceremonies from the U. of I., and a war with its attendant disruptions throughout the country had interfered with everyone's life. In 1952 the California Alpha chapter of Tau Beta Pi honored recent recipients at their annual banquet in Lafayette. Logan was also inducted there into the Illinois Alpha chapter. Throughout his professional life he wore the Tau Beta Pi tie chain at appropriate functions, a subtle yet recognizable reminder of the honor bestowed.

At home, our young sons were two and four. The eight-year-old house we rented in Carmichael had a little more space inside, and 22 Valencia orange trees on its half acre. On a clear day one could see the snow-capped Sierra Nevada from the east window. The house had a bath and a half, three bedrooms, a sunny living-dining area and two levels. But many things needed repair.

For a year as tenant Logan quietly considered the home's assets and liabilities. The materials used had been the last available before WWII limited home-building supplies, and some unproven plastics were used here and there. Also, whoever built the house probably assumed that, being on a slight hill, drainage would be no problem. But that was a wrong assumption. However, Logan decided the problems were solvable and we made an offer on the house, which was accepted.

Beneath the soil about a foot, more or less, was a layer of impenetrable hard-pan. No water was absorbed through that layer. When the winter rains came, water accumulated in the crawl-space under the house. This put out the floor furnace pilot light and was unhealthy at best. Logan solved the problem by installing drain tiles around the perimeter of the house to carry the water away from the structure and down toward the road.

He painted the house and had a new septic system installed. Inside he put in a new kitchen sink drain connected to the new septic system. He cut the Bermuda grass with a gasoline-powered cutter attachment on a cultivator. *"It's a widow-maker,"* he said as he wiped the sweat from his brow. He had the driveway paved and planted A*belia Edward Goucher* around the septic tank. He pruned the valencia orange trees to improve their productivity. We drank gallons of orange juice. With a tall antenna we could pull in, from the Bay Area, the only availableTV stations at that time. From an upstairs window our eyes were trained patiently toward Nevada whenever trial nuclear explosions were scheduled to be detonated. Each Christmas we decorated a live Deodar tree for our living room, and later planted it in the yard. When all these things were accomplished, it was truly a comfortable, livable home in which to raise our two growing boys and their dog.

One might wonder, is anything wrong with this situation? We now had a comfortable home. Logan was often out in the field and had the opportunity to visit rugged parts of the state, coupled with engineering for which he had been trained. He seemed to enjoy this for over three years, while I was busy with homemaking activities. At work he occasionally locked horns with the state bureaucracy. The event that finally triggered his resignation might have seemed minor to an observer, but to Logan, raised in frugality and the straight-forward assessment and solution of problems, it was a signal event.

His surveyors were assigned to go to these remote potential parks, lay out their survey lines, and plot improvements for public convenience. To accomplish this they needed survey stakes--not huge quantities, just enough to do the job. The most logical approach would be to buy the stakes at a local supply store in the area of the work. They could purchase only what they needed, do the job, and prepare for the next assignment. Job done. Proceed to the next job—buy the stakes,do the job, etc. But that was too simple for the state.

Someone in an office somewhere said the purchase of the stakes had to be put out to bid and purchased from the lowest bidder. This may have sounded good to that Someone in the office. But there were other factors: store the huge quantity of purchased stakes (pay for renting space); estimate how many of those stakes were needed for the jobs (office calculations & memos); load a truck (manpower) with the required stakes for several weeks on the road (bigger vehicle); cart the stakes to the site where needed (bigger vehicle, more fuel); etc., etc. The local supplier might charge a bit more per stake, but the overhead involved in the State's method far exceeded the cost of purchasing only the required stakes from a local supplier. What's more, there was no estimate of the time saved and convenience. The local goodwill generated by purchasing stakes in the area was an unmeasurable item. The State, of course, had its rules and wouldn't—or couldn't—budge.

Logan's practical side told him he couldn't operate with the frustrations of such a system. By this time he knew Tim Train as one of his best surveyors. Tim, too, chafed under the state's procedures, and they decided to pool their resources and go into business. In the spring of 1953 they were honored at a farewell luncheon. Earl Hansen, the deputy chief of the Division, was present with suitable accolades, as well as co-workers from the office and the field. Logan and Tim departed to set up Muir & Train in downtown Sacramento in the Mitau Building at 8th and Jay Streets. It was a professional engineering and land surveying firm, ready to do business with any public or private entity for whom they could provide services.

CHAPTER 12—A BUSINESS LAUNCHED
Out of the Ball Park

When private men shall act with original views, the luster will be transferred
– Ralph Waldo Emerson

It is necessary to briefly envision the enthusiasm and optimism that was sweeping across the country after World War II. With the war over, there was no end to the opportunities available for anyone willing to grasp the brass ring as this civilian merry-go-round picked up momentum. Those who had their schooling interrupted by war were eager to complete their educations. The government passed the GI bill, one part of which gave financial assistance to veterans who wished to go to college. Before the war campuses were made up largely of unmarried students. After the war the colleges created family housing for students who brought a wife and kids along.

Sacramento had one major engineering firm. Joe Spink and his engineers had been there for some time, and their prominence in the community was undisputed and unchallenged. But with the burgeoning population and the need for housing in the area, perhaps there would be room for another firm to take some of the "overflow". Joe welcomed the newcomers. He even helped them in an unexpected way early on.

Everyone wanted to be a homeowner, it seemed. The subdivision business was waiting to boom, and Muir and Train assessed this situation. Housing developments, roads, sewer lines, plot plans—all those things their new firm could provide. Logan's and Tim's confidence would carry them over for a time. That, and about $2000. which they each invested in the firm, plus the use of their own cars.

Muir and Train's one room in the Mitau Building at 8th and Jay Streets was bare except for a telephone, a few pieces of furniture, and the usual engineering office equipment. One day both Logan and Tim had to be out of the office for the entire day, and I volunteered to answer the phone for them. At that time cell-phones were unknown. I sat in their modest office all day keeping our young sons busy with desk-type projects. The phone didn't ring even once.

At home we had lean times as our few remaining savings went to the business. We ate a lot of beanie-wienie and found ways to be frugal so the fledgling firm could stay afloat. It would be awhile before either of the principals could take home a salary.

Public Relations (PR) is taken for granted today, but that costs money, a scarce and expensive commodity for Muir and Train. When their firm began, both the *Sacramento Bee* and the *Sacramento Union* gave them good coverage. That was a start.

One day Logan read in the newspaper about a homerun hit the day before by Sacramento Solon outfielder Neill Sheridan at Edmonds Field in Sacramento. The article suggested that it might have been the longest homerun in baseball history.

Logan jumped at the opportunity to have his survey crews officially measure the distance. He would certify their accuracy with his professional engineer's stamp. What followed were a series of news articles and comments that gave the young unknown business the kind of publicity that many firms would be willing to purchase.

(...from the *Sacramento Union*, July 13, 1953 ...)
*SHERIDAN HOMER CHECKS OUT AT 613.8
FEET*

*Neill Sheridan's bid for the longest home run ever hit by
mortal man was made official yesterday!
The surveying firm of Muir & Train took its instruments
to Edmonds Field and made an accurate measurement
which placed the distance at 613.80 feet.*

*Logan N. Muir, Jr., a civil engineer, and Timothy S.
Train, a land surveyor, said they will prepare an official
plot of Sheridan's home run, from home plate to the spot it
landed in Pat Kelly's auto parked on Burnett Way.*

> *The official 613.80 feet is approximately six feet shorter*
> *than the original claim of 620 feet, the latter being made*
> *on the basis of tape measuring done by groundskeeper*
> *Horace Smith.*

> *Nevertheless it is 13.80 feet longer than the distance*
> *credited to Babe Ruth years ago when he is supposed to*
> *have hit the record homer of all time in an exhibition*
> *game at Tampa, Florida. Frank G. Menke's* Encyclopedia
> of Sports *credits the Babe with 600 feet.*

> *Further authenticity to Sheridan's homer came yesterday*
> *when it was revealed that one of the employees working*
> *in the Edmonds Field parking lot heard the impact of*
> *shattered glass when the epic circuit clout soared over the*
> *left wall and entered Kelly's parked auto by way of the rear*
> *window.*

People who were interested in such things began talking about it during their lunch hour, or over cocktails, or wherever they gathered. It was not a big topic, but more news articles followed, which kept the story alive. As the firm gradually began to prosper, an occasional contact in the business world would brighten up and say, *"Oh, you're the guys that measured that home run."* It was always a conversation starter at least, and the word began to get around. Even three years later a reverberation in the Peoria, Illinois, *Journal Star* questioning the validity of the distance received this letter from Logan. It was also published in the Sacramento *Union*.

> *Sports Editor,*
> *Peoria Journal-Star*
> *Peoria, Illinois*

> *Dear Sir: A huge, malignant shadow drifted across*
> *Sacramento today causing men to tremble, women*
> *to weep, and babes to stir in their cribs, for word has*
> *reached Sacramento of an article in your esteemed paper*
> *introducing for the first time anywhere the word "IF" into*

the saga of Neill Sheridan's record home run wallop.

*Sir, it is as though you were a Pied Piper of print, piping
all our dreams of glory and pride of local accomplishment
out of Sacramento forever. You say "if the ball didn't
bounce." Sir, no-one, yea, no-one SAW the ball bounce.*

*Your cruel suggestion casts this shadow of doubt on all
manufacturers; the manufacturers of sloping rear windows
of cars; the Sacramento Solons together with all their
players and all their players' mothers; Neill Sheridan
and his country; the oldest and best newspaper west of
someplace west of Peoria, The Sacramento <u>Union,</u> and
its entire staff and their mothers; Muir and Train and
the manufacturers of their equipment; Mayor Clarence
Azevedo of Sacramento and all of the City and of the
County of Sacramento—all of these, dear sir, are maligned
by that little word of distrust, that torpedo that sinks the
good ship "Faith," that monstrous, dastardly, scurrilous
little word "if."*

*An', Sor, ye've done worse than that, fer sure an y've shtruck
at th' luck o' the Irish. Fer wosn't it a Sheridan as belted
the boll the width o' County Cork? An' wosn't it a Kelley
as was shpielin' publicity fer the Solons? And anither Kelly
'twas whose car window wos broken t'smithereens, and
thin agin, faith, 'twas a Conlin who is afther bein' Sports
Editor of The Union, who first writ the tale, an' thin
begorra 'twas me own partner Timothy as measured the
613.8 feet!*

*So I say, let the record be 613.8 feet. Let the sun shine
again in Sacramento. It will not shine the less in Peoria
for such generosity! After all, with no reflections on the
mighty Babe, that 600-foot figure is all too round and
even a figure to ever have been measured at all.*

> *And so, Mr., Sports Editor, let's raise a glass and rejoice in*
> *America and American mothers that produce a son who*
> *can hit that old apple 613.8 feet that nobody saw bounce!*

> *Sincerely,*
> */S/ Logan N. Muir, Jr*

Business was picking up, but not yet enough for the principals to glean a livable salary. A strike in the building industry dealt them a blow as subdivision work came to a standstill. They kept––and paid––their two valued surveyors, Artie Roecker and Clint Calvert, and found related survey work for them, even if the firm got no payment for their efforts. I wanted to help somehow, and with that thought applied for a job with the USGS working as a cartographer. I had no experience, but was hired on a Friday to draw contour lines shown on geological maps. The job would begin the following Monday.

The week-end gave us time to think and talk over the wisdom of the job. In effect, my entire university education would be ignored. And where would our two young sons be cared for? There was a better solution, but it meant further delay in any income. We decided that, instead of drawing maps, I would go to Sacramento State College [now Sacramento State University] to earn the 30 or more units for a teaching credential. As a teacher I could have roughly the same year-round schedule as our sons who were nearing school age. We would have more belt tightening, but perhaps better times were ahead. Our viewpoint was always positive, and we didn't dwell unrealistically on imaginary problems.

Developers were often operating on a shoe string, and frequently needed reminders that they owed the firm money. Collecting money was not engineering work, but in a small firm, the principals had to cover all their bases and stay on top of the cash flow.

One day I offered to help, and Logan reluctantly gave me the name of "Otto" for whom their surveyors had completed work some time before. Their hope of getting paid was dwindling. Our two young sons went with me as I tracked down Otto out on a job somewhere and requested that he pay for the work done. He probably looked at our two boys and me and did come through with a partial payment. My efforts were minimal, but Logan was quick to give me credit. Credit also goes to our sons, Andy and Al, who seemed to accept our financial struggles without complaining and often took on responsibilities beyond their years.

Bob Powell, their Registered Engineer in charge of land planning between 1954 and 1956, helped in another way: with confidence in Muir and Train, he quietly held his pay checks until such time as the firm began to prosper.

Joe Spink knew of the struggles of the new firm and gave Muir and Train office calculations for his firm's engineering and surveying jobs. It was more than minor help for this struggling firm. It was useful work, and remuneration was dependable.

One of Muir and Train's early jobs was a subdivision of about 30 lots on El Camino Avenue. Logan and Tim spread out their maps on the coffee table and it was evident from their enthusiasm that they relished the chance to get their teeth into a real project.

By late 1954 engineering and surveying jobs were picking up, but developers were slow to pay. It was evident that Logan and Tim would need the money from their home equities to support the business. We sold our home—and Tim sold his—and moved into Sacramento, leaving behind the orange grove and our comfortable home with a view of the snow-capped Sierra Nevada. Our rented home in town was temporary and by mid-1955 I was hired by the Sacramento City Unified School District. We now had a modest steady income of about $400. a month.

Eastern Heights near El Camino Avenue was one of Muir and Train's subdivisions. One of the best parcels in it was still on the market. It had a new 3-bedroom house with 2 baths, and a graceful old native oak tree in the back yard. The potential buyer did not qualify for a loan, and we purchased it with the government's GI bill available at that time, requiring no down payment. In addition, new schools were being built in the subdivision, and our sons would be settled into classrooms that were not crowded and temporary.

Very gradually the firm of Muir and Train became known around town. Both partners joined their professional organizations, and for Logan this included, among others, the national, state, and local chapters of the Society of Professional Engineers. It's likely that he stopped the absurd idea of asking newly registered engineers to clear the tables after a dinner meeting.

He soon became an officer in a number of professional organizations, sometimes starting out as secretary, a menial job which meant a lot of note-taking and record keeping. But it was an opportunity to understand the aims and functions of the organization, and to meet other engineers. He served in those capacities with distinction, and was subsequently rewarded with posts as vice-president and then president. Always, when the opportunity arose, he emphasized that the title of Professional Engineer (P.E.) carried with it a trust to serve the public.

CHAPTER 13—THE NAVAL RESERVE
Classified Orders

He serves me most, who serves his country best.
— **Alexander Pope**

In order to review Logan's naval service it is necessary to look back in time and focus on 1945. World War II ended in September of that year. Navy ships and servicemen were returning from overseas in increasing numbers. Seabees were discharged at Camp Parks near Pleasanton, first in small numbers, and then in ever-larger numbers. As for Logan, by November he was scheduled to be separated from active duty in the Navy and received this letter from Captain Randig thanking him for his service:

CONSTRUCTION BATTALION REPLACEMENT DEPOT

Camp Parks, Shoemaker, California
26 November 1945

My Dear Muir:

On the occasion of your transfer from the Construction Battalion Replacement Depot, Camp Parks to a separation center for processing to inactive duty, I desire to express my appreciation for the service which you have rendered to the Navy in general and to this station in particular in time of war.

During the period of time you have been aboard you have brought credit to the Naval Service by the efficient performance of your duty as Assistant to Public Works Officer from 25 November 1944 to 26 November 1945.

*The performance of your collateral assignment as Member
Board for Changes in Ratings was done in exemplary
fashion.*

*It is my hope that you will meet with every success on your
return to civilian life.*

*Sincerely yours
[S] W. H. Randig
Captain, CEC, USN
Acting Civil Engineer Officer in Command*

In late December, 1945, this letter arrived from James Forrestal, Secretary of the Navy. It sums up the accomplishments of the Navy during WWII.

My dear Mr. Muir:

*I have addressed this letter to reach you after all the
formalities of your separation from active service are
completed. I have done so because without formality but
as clearly as I know how to say it, I want the Navy's pride
in you, which it is my privilege to express, to reach into
your civil life and to remain with you always.*

*You have served in the greatest Navy in the world.
It crushed two enemy fleets at once, receiving their
surrenders only four months apart.*

*It brought our land-based airpower within bombing range
of the enemy, and set our ground armies on the beachheads
of final victory.*

*It performed the multitude of tasks necessary to support
these military operations.*

*No other Navy at any time has done so much. For your
part in these achievements you deserve to be proud as long*

*as you live. The Nation which you served at a time of crisis
will remember you with gratitude.*

*The best wishes of the Navy go with you into civilian life.
Good luck!*

*Sincerely yours,
/S/ James Forrestal*

In 1946 the war's end was still fresh in everyone's thoughts. Some men
were glad to be out of uniform and once again pick up their civilian lives
interrupted by war. Some were mindful of the continuing need for a strong
military readiness in an unsettled post-war world. Logan was in this latter
group. Though employed in a civilian job [with the David D. Bohannon
Organization], Logan kept his affiliation with the Navy and joined a Naval
Reserve unit in the Bay area. When we moved to Sacramento in 1950 he
continued his Navy commitment with a reserve unit there.

He was diligent about attending the weekly training sessions. Before
leaving home, everything about his uniform was scrutinized—Naval
insignia militarily correct, shoes shined to a mirror polish, ribbons
carefully placed, creases just so—and he was ready for any inspection.
He also carried with him all necessary papers for that particular training
session. En route in full uniform during the summer months the
western sun beat relentlessly into his car. It was probably the only part
of this duty that he dreaded, but he accepted it along with the serious
responsibilities involved.

In order to remain in the Reserves, the Navy required its personnel
to attend two weeks of active training duty annually. The purpose was
to keep abreast of the latest and newest Navy activities, trends, and
technology, and to strengthen the involvement of the Reserves. The
ability to be ready for active duty was an important part of the larger
mission. Logan invited me along occasionally to give me a two-week
vacation from homemaking while cheerful grandparents baby-sat. For
me it was another opportunity to see more of this interesting state.

In the mid-1950s Logan's two weeks of active Navy duty was his only
time away from the pressing duties of his young, struggling business. He
looked forward to those two weeks and the change of pace which the
Navy provided. Sometimes he arrived home from such service with only

a few pennies in his pocket. But he also carried a check for the two weeks' duty—a welcome and often necessary addition to the family purse.

His diligence and availability did not go unnoticed. The Navy at that time had––and perhaps still has––a point system. Points were given for training duty attendance, for correspondence courses completed, for willingness to serve, and for dedication to the Navy's mission. With Logan's promotions along the way, his points toward retirement accumulated.

During the Viet Nam conflict in the mid-1960s, he was asked if he would be willing to return to active duty if called. The world was unsettled and Logan was willing to do whatever his country asked to ensure a successful conclusion to events in the Pacific. He replied in the affirmative, though it would have meant hardship for his business.

He was issued, and carried always, a classified card which told him that, if ordered, he was to proceed within 48 hours and report to the Public Works Office in Pearl Harbor, Hawaii, "bumping" any airline passenger if necessary. Except for certain Navy personnel, he and I were the only civilians who knew of this card. Though he was not re-called to active duty, he was always ready during the uncertain world events at that time.

In 1965 a Naval Reserve Counseling Board was established to assist officers who were leaving active duty to keep abreast of duty commitments and promotion requirements. The board served the entire Sacramento Valley area. According to the *Sacramento Bee* (September 16, 1965), Captain Muir was one of eight officers who met twice weekly, counseling officers to get in touch with reserve units compatible with their specialties.

In 1968 the country was becoming divided about the Viet Nam conflict. To put events into perspective Logan sent the following letter:

> *The Honorable Wayne Morse*
> *United States Senator*
> *Senate Office Building*
> *Washington, D.C. 20025*
>
> *Dear Senator Morse:*
>
> *I have just heard your statements on NBC radio following the adoption of the majority plank on Viet Nam by the Democratic Convention.*

I am sure you are wrong when you state the majority of people in the United States are in favor of pulling out of Viet Nam. Rather, such people are in a noisy, emotional, irrational minority. An example of such irrationality is your own emphasis on 'American Boys' being slaughtered in Viet Nam.
In the first place, they are men and not 'boys'— valiant ones at that.

Second, if it's slaughter you're opposed to, I suggest you direct your attention and intelligence to traffic deaths in the United States, where twice the number of Americans are slaughtered <u>each year</u> as in the entire time of the Viet Nam war.

Further, it is not only men who are slaughtered on our highways, but 'boys', girls, women, and the elderly.

And further, what can be more immoral than death due to drunkenness, carelessness, negligence, and incompetence!

So wipe away the crocodile tears, Senator, and try to stand bravely up to the responsibilities that mature men and mature nations must face. You will then and only then be on the side of a majority of Americans.

Sincerely,
/S/ Logan Muir, PE
cc: President Johnson

Logan's commitment to the Navy was firm. He never wavered in his dedication to the Navy and fulfillment of all necessary obligations commensurate with rank. Perhaps the late President John F. Kennedy expressed it best when he said, *"Ask not what your country can do for you—ask what you can do for your country."*

Long before that statement was on everyone's lips, Logan had already made his own commitment.

CHAPTER 14—THE BUSINESS GROWS
A Chinaman's Chance

An honest business never blush to tell.
– Alexander Pope

Engineer's Week was celebrated in Sacramento during the week including February 22, George Washington's birth date. Our first president was a land surveyor by profession and his early contributions to land surveying in his home state of Virginia were a focal point of the week.

During Engineers' Week in February, 1955, engineers from the Department of Water Resources, the Redevelopment Agency, SMUD (the Sacramento Municipal Utility District), and the City of Sacramento were invited on various local TV shows to discuss the engineering profession and its importance to the public. As a member of the private sector Logan was invited to be on a panel on KCRA-TV. This put him and Muir & Train further into the public eye.

At that time the business was still in its early stages and we were living temporarily in a rented house on Berkeley Way in Sacramento. After work Logan occasionally poured himself a cocktail and began sipping it in the living room where he watched the news while I started dinner preparations in the kitchen. I knew of Logan's possible later appearance on KCRA, probably in connection with Engineers' Week, but didn't know when it would be.

One day he called to me to join him in the living room. I replied that I'd be there as soon as I had dinner preparations underway. His second call was more urgent, and I decided the dinner preparations could wait. I arrived in the living room just as the TV showed a reporter at an engineers' luncheon making his way around the luncheon table and asking selected engineers the same pertinent question: *"What is your impression of the shorter skirts that are the new fashion for women today?"*

Some of the engineers briefly said they liked them or didn't like them, and the reporter moved on around the table. Logan's answer was a bit different, and received more coverage on the evening television news. His reply: *"As an engineer, I'm always interested in structures, and the shorter skirts are an aid in that direction."*

It was the late 1950's. As business picked up and responsibilities and obligations increased, Muir and Train incorporated with Luke Packard's firm, Aeromap Surveys, to form Packard, Muir & Train, Inc. Aeromap Surveys had been engaged in topographic mapping using aerial and photogrammetric methods. Muir and Train was in the general practice of civil engineering and land surveying, and the two businesses complemented each other in services provided. Around town the firm became known informally as PMT. They were no competition for the Joe Spink civil engineering firm, but PMT was beginning to make a name for itself.

Before construction of a subdivision, plans had to be presented to and passed by the local planning commission, which had the ability to accept or reject them, or request changes before approval. PMT's representative who presented such plans was Lincoln Ong, a sharp employee who was already known to the commission members from his earlier appearances.

One evening Lincoln was at a planning commission meeting that dragged on and on with haggling and wrangling on all sides. It was after 10:00 p.m. before they finally got to PMT's subdivision on the agenda. Everyone was exhausted, not in the best of moods, and wanted to get out of there and go home.

Lincoln stepped up to the podium and said, *"I don't suppose I have a Chinaman's chance of getting this passed tonight."* The tension in the room melted in laughter, a gavel approved the plans without question, and the meeting was adjourned.

This was not blind approval. By that time PMT had a reputation for complete and accurate engineering and surveying. Rarely did a problem develop with plans submitted by their firm. If a problem did develop later, every effort was professionally made by PMT to correct it. This, plus the involvement of the principals in local engineering societies and events, gave them recognition in the engineering community and in the public eye. Their name was trusted.

In the early 1960's we found a large old home for sale on 38th Street in Sacramento. It was only a few blocks from Logan's office at 33rd and Jay Streets, and if we lived there he could enjoy walking to work.

It would also shorten my commute to Peter Lassen Junior High. At that time our family also needed more space—our teen-age sons were growing, each with his own interests, and there was the real probability that Logan's mother would soon be living with us.

The house was built about 1915 and had been partitioned into smaller living quarters during the World War II housing shortage. There were accoustic ceilings in the living room, several gas jets formerly used for lighting upstairs and down, and a built-in decorative cabinet in the dining room where glassware and china could be displayed. It needed many renovations, particularly in the kitchen, to bring it up to code, but had the potential to be the lovely old spacious home it once was. Our offer on the house was accepted, and our family then enjoyed the challenges and opportunities that this new/old house gave us.

Packard, Muir & Train was gradually growing. On week-ends we often drove around the area to inspect PMT's on-going engineering and land surveying subdivision projects in the Sacramento area. The work was done by employees, and Logan's inspection and subsequent civil engineering stamp on the plans gave final approval.

Subdividers were often slow to pay and usually the best payers were government agencies or utilities. At that time the *PG&E Progress* was a newsletter inserted with each gas bill sent to customers. In May, 1961, the front-page article was about the use of a Geodimeter to survey a potential pipe-line. The pipeline would carry natural gas to Morro Bay for use in generating electricity. Excerpts from the article which gave additional publicity to PMT follow:

> *...the survey crews were rarely seen by residents or travelers since much of the work was performed at night...these men relied largely on an electronic timing device capable of extreme accuracy... Because the Geodimeter utilizes a beam of specialized light, it is used to best advantage at night...[it] operates at distances up to 5 miles... [It cuts] conventional survey costs as much as 40%...Packard, Muir & Train, Inc., of Sacramento, did the work for PG&E under contract.*

Other publicity came when the <u>Sacramento Union's</u> Kurt MacBride gave the firm seven lines of publicity about the Morro Bay job in his daily column. Clearly, PMT was becoming known in the Sacramento area.

With Packard, Muir & Train's business at 33rd and Jay Street Logan could often walk home at noon, read the mail, and eat a simple lunch. It was a quiet opportunity to think through some of the tangled problems he encountered in his business before returning to work refreshed.

It was May and the teachers at Peter Lassen planned a last family pot-luck picnic before beginning those final crowded weeks of exams and grades. My contribution would be a salad, and the evening before, I created a molded gelatin concoction. I thought it looked appealing even as it gelled in the refrigerator. The next morning I took one more approving look at the salad before leaving for school. The plan was to return after school, pick up the family and the salad, and head for the picnic spot.

After school I looked at the salad in the refrigerator, expecting to admire it one more time before wrapping it for the supper.

My heart sank! A chunk was removed from one corner! Could someone in our hungry family have sampled it? Almost immediately I noticed a greeting card neatly tucked nearby with this bit of Logan-inspired rhyme written in it:

> *The reason for my ballad is*
> *I dipped into the salad*
> *'Fore I 'membered what you'd made it for.*
>
> *Now you can tell the teachers*
> *You've a household full of reachers*
> *And your husband's just a big old hungry boar.*
>
> *Better yet — you tell 'em*
> *So's the salad wouldn't fell 'em*
> *I tested it and found it safe to life.*
>
> *They can eat it without fearing*
> *Their stomach lining's searing*
> *The salad didn't kill me — it's my wife!*

This was vintage Logan at home: not a straight-forward grovelling apology, but making the best of a situation, a little humility, and ending with a final ridiculous spin. Maybe he did marry me because I laughed at his jokes. I filled in the missing part with suitable garnishes. At the family picnic no one seemed to notice that someone had sampled it before it was brought to the table.

In the early 1960s our sons were attending Sutter Junior High School in Sacramento and I was still teaching at Peter Lassen. In the spring the city schools held open house to give students an opportunity to display their accomplishments and parents could talk briefly with the teachers. My presence at Peter Lassen Junior High prevented me from attending Sutter Junior High as a parent, but Logan went there and participated in the open house activities. After one such evening Logan felt compelled to draft this response to a talk he heard at Sutter. The article is a work in progress and was never sent, probably because of pressing duties in his business.

Atomic Scientist, Everyone?

Earlier this month, parents of Sutter Junior High students were privileged to hear Dr. Albert Sessarego, principal of Sacramento High School, in a discussion of the scope and aims of the curriculum available at his school.

Dr. Sessarego is an intelligent, enthusiastic and extremely capable educator who good-humoredly acknowledges that Sacramento High School is the best in the entire world.

He explained that there is today a greater emphasis on science and mathematics in the schools than at any time since the war.

He does not feel that this is necessarily all to the good. He feels that the world may yet be saved by the sociologist, the philosophers, the statesmen.

The engineer and scientist are often blamed for the present state of affairs because they have created such terrible weapons as the arrow, the arbalest, and the atomic bomb. Unfortunately, these and many other great scientific developments received the greatest impetus in their development during struggles for survival under understandingly compelling circumstances. Even scientists have been unnecessarily remorseful of their own efforts in this respect.

But the truth of the matter is that the scientific principles involved in all these terrifying applications provide much more potential promise for the good of man than for his doom. Scientific principles are neither moral nor immoral, virtuous nor sinful, political nor non-political. But who is it that puts these principles to use? Yes, it is politicians (shall we say political scientists?) and statesmen (let's guard against the use of "Diplomacy Engineers"!). And who, in a democracy, sanctions the activities of the statesman and the politician? Why it's the people!

It's the people – the very people – that Dr. Sessarego is educating. It is the people who are the parents of those he is educating. It is the sociologist, the philosophers, the English teachers, and all the rest of us.

So, to properly evaluate the activities of our elected representatives and leaders, to sanction or censure them, all of our people need to be educated to understand the good and bad of scientific principles and the possible impact of these developments on our lives and the lives of our children. And our leaders, representatives, and experts likewise must know something about, not just of, science.

No, not everyone can be or wants to be an atomic scientist. But our people and their leaders must have the knowledge to enable them to make intelligent and sound appraisals of the many wonderful things that science and engineering will provide. For these can be the means to a better, fuller life, to the solution of the problems of today and tomorrow and to everlasting peace if we will it so. There can be no greater goal for education.

Don't you agree, Dr. Sessarego?

Logan N. Muir, Jr., P.E.

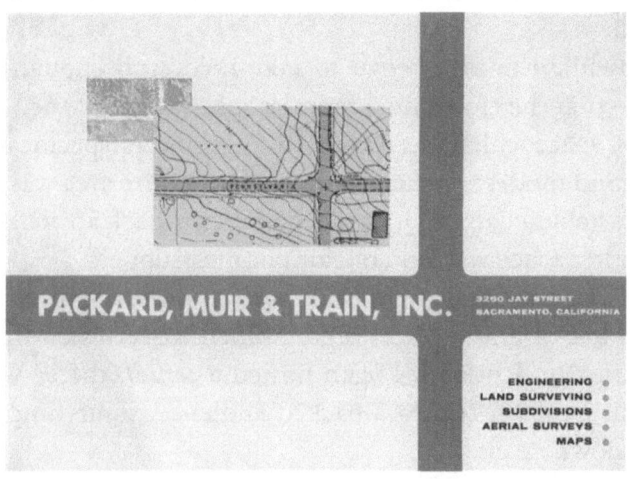

PACKARD, MUIR & TRAIN, INC. 3290 JAY STREET
SACRAMENTO, CALIFORNIA

ENGINEERING
LAND SURVEYING
SUBDIVISIONS
AERIAL SURVEYS
MAPS

This brochure (cover shown here) was given to potential clients

By 1964 the firm was doing better financially. We added up the figures and were surprised to discover that my added income pushed us into a higher tax bracket. I was, in effect, working for less than the minimum wage. We reasoned that I could be more effective at home, particularly assisting Logan in his professional endeavors. So I retired from teaching in 1964 to devote my full attention to our home and family.

Logan had often thought seriously about starting an Engineers' Club in Sacramento. He knew that San Francisco, for example, had a comfortable Engineers' Club in the city, where engineers could find respite from their daily obligations and meet and talk over engineering problems with other engineers in a casual setting, away from the pressure of their busy schedules.

Logan looked around town and he (and probably a few other like-minded engineers) thought the top floor of the Elks Building would be a great spot for beginning an engineer's club. It was at that time the tallest building in town and the view from there looking out over the city was a lovely quiet experience. It would be a modest start but he hoped to get engineers in the habit of talking with each other about mutual problems in an informal setting. And that's how the Last Friday of the Month Club began. I assisted Logan at that time and a different theme was carried out each month. It all began very slowly until word began to get around in the engineering community that something was going on there.

After awhile the idea began to take hold, and enough engineers backed it so that the club rented roomier space at one of the Elks Club's lower floors, space which was renovated to engineers' specifications with rest rooms and modest kitchen facilities. One entire area was furnished with comfortable chairs that could be pushed back to make a dance floor. Another space was suitable for pot-luck suppers.

Several evening meals were held there, and the engineering groups began to think of it as a place to go. When we returned from one of our early trips to Scotland, Logan hosted a *ceilidh* there. We showed slides of our Scottish trip to a packed audience, something we could have done nowhere else.

*   *   *   *   *   *   *

Several of the principals in PMT were pilots in World War II, and in the 1960s they convinced the firm to invest in an airplane and expand the territory of its engineering and surveying services into other western states. Not to be out-flown, as it were, Logan decided to learn to fly also. One day he came home from work with news: *"My first in-flight lesson will be next Thursday..."* The enthusiasm in his voice was echoed in mine: I agreed that this was a marvelous idea. Then came a surprise.

"...and yours is next Wednesday!" Logan often returned home with news of an interesting event of the day to share. But this development was beyond anything I could have imagined.

We went to ground school together and learned all about the pre-flight inspection, rudders, ailerons, wings, carburetor heat, ground speed, air speed and pitot tubes, stalling, and a multitude of other details that a pilot must know before solo flying is permitted. We each took in-flight lessons with flight instructor Orville Nelson at the Patterson Aircraft Company. Logan flew in PMT's 205 Cessna, 8466Z, and I was in a rented 150 Cessna, usually 4396U. For many days I concentrated and rewrote, over and over again, the pre-flight procedures for take-off and the exact sequence of steps for landing until the order was firmly fixed in my mind.

Taking off is relatively easy. The plane wants to fly. It almost tells you so as you wait for clearance from the control tower. Bringing it back to earth safely is quite another matter. Orville came along as I practiced touch and go landings at Franklin Field south of Sacramento. Over and over again: a full-throttle climb off the runway, level off, bank left, fly downwind, and set up the landing. Stated simply, that was the routine. Again and again. Orville critiqued each circuit when necessary, often saying simply, "*Take it around again.*" Always he was helpful and patient.

One day after this concentrated practice, Orville asked me to bring the plane to a stop at the side of the landing strip. "*Take it around,*" he said matter-of-factly. "*Watch for me as you set up your landing...*" I felt ready to solo, but at that time it was a mystery how he, too, knew the exact moment when I was ready. He climbed out of the plane and left me alone.

Few things before or since have quite matched the thrill of being alone in that plane for the first time. Would I remember everything: to cut back the throttle, to bank–but not too steeply, to make a gentle turn to go downwind, to turn on carburetor heat, and—probably most important of all—to put all the details together to land safely?

The first solo was successful. Orville didn't flag me to stop, but waved me around again. Three times I brought the plane back safely, and he endorsed my license for solo flights, carrying no passengers. Logan was ahead of me on the calendar. He soloed earlier, and was already doing cross country solo flights.

Landing successfully is of utmost importance, and even though one can solo, landing practice goes on and on. We practiced at Franklin Field where there was no control tower. On at least one occasion Logan and I were there at the same time, each practicing touch and go. The firm's Cessna "205" is a more-powerful and faster plane than the "150", and care had to be taken that we didn't collide as we concentrated on landing. We rarely talked to each other by radio, but finally he came on the radio and said he was heading back to Sacramento. I agreed to follow him, but by that time I couldn't see his plane and had no idea where he was in the air. I called the Sacramento Tower, probably in a panic.

"*Where's my traffic? Where's my traffic?*" The controller in the tower knew both of us, and at that point the Tower and I were both searching the sky for 8466Zulu. Silence, at first, and then broken by this brief transmission from Logan: "*Gee! A man can't even get away from his wife up here!*" He was already preparing to set up his landing at the airport. It was all good fun, exhilarating and demanding, as we prepared for the pilot's license test.

Logan's serious mind easily carried him through flying lessons

In Logan's last session before the final test, he and Orville were flying cross-country, and I was invited along as a passenger. The Cessna 205 has two gas tanks, and the pilot was expected to understand that, if the engine stopped, he should first switch to the other tank and find out if he had run out of gas. When Orville quietly reached down and turned off the gas tank, the engine sputtered to a stop. He expected Logan to set up an emergency landing somewhere.

With barely a moment's thought Logan reached down for the lever and switched gas tanks. Orville laughed mildly and said, "*Well, where would you land if you had run out of gas?*" Logan was well prepared for the final test and received his private pilot's license on November 9, 1965.

My efforts at piloting a plane were less successful. When the instructor put me "under the hood", a part of the test which teaches you to trust your instruments, I was uncomfortable and wanted to see the real horizon. Even after solo cross-country practice trips to Napa, Santa

Rosa and other fields, the license eluded me. However, my consolation is that, at that time, I believed I could handle a small-plane landing—and survive—if the pilot became incapacitated.

The airplane expanded the scope of PMT's business. Trips were made into other western states—Idaho, Montana, Nevada, Wyoming, Oregon—where engineering and surveying jobs were found. In order to perform engineering in those states, registration was required. Often it was given by reciprocity, based on California's reputation of high qualifications and standards for professional engineering registration.

By this time Logan was often asked to speak at a luncheon or dinner event. One group who asked him was the Sacramento chapter of C.S.P.E. It was thought worthy of printing in the *California Professional Engineer,* and it was also reprinted later in an edition of the *Western I.T.E.* (Institute of Traffic Engineers) newsletter:

> *Logan Muir on Professionalism*
>
> *Speaking before the Sacramento Chapter of CSPE at its January meeting, Logan N.Muir, Jr., P.E., member of the firm Packard, Muir & Train addressed himself to the topic, "Is Engineering Really a Profession?" After presenting several definitions of professionalism, including that of the Taft-Hartley Act, he provided the following descriptive terms and suggested that the listeners ask themselves how engineering and engineers measure up:*
>
> *First, character – This is the general reliability of an individual to act in conformity to duty. Does he put service above gain, excellence above quantity, self-expression above pecuniary motives, and loyalty above individual advantage? What are his ideas and what is his state of mind?*
>
> *Next, technical knowledge and competence – Is he technically well educated both by schooling and experience and does he keep his knowledge up-dated by additional formal schooling, by association with knowledgeable*

people, by reading, by experimentation? Does he apply this knowledge competently, with thoroughness, realistically?

Then, breadth of knowledge and ability to communicate – is he a mere technical specialist? Does he know and attempt to understand what is going on in his community, the nation, and the world? Has he learned about people, their hopes, desires, aspirations? Their fears, weaknesses and foibles? Can he talk and write and convey ideas? And how about tolerance, understanding and respect – Does he understand and respect his fellow professionals, other professions, his neighbor, his congressman, the institutions of his government? Does he tolerate and attempt to understand other points of view than his own, other interpretations, other opinions?

As to leadership – is he willing to express a considered opinion, to lead a fight to achieve a determined end, to compromise for the sake of achievement?

How about creativity – Is he a copy-cat or does he strive constantly to improve a method or a process? Is he afraid of innovation or is he always searching to make a breakthrough? Does he try to develop a sense for good taste and aesthetics or is he satisfied with the humdrum, the ordinary, the uninteresting?

Registration, he said, is not professionalism although it is a step in that direction. Registration is the bottom rung on the professional ladder. It measures only technical competence—not devotion to duty and ideals, not tolerance and understanding, not leadership or creativity – and it measures only the minimum acceptable technical competency.

Concluding, he said, My score card says engineering <u>really can be</u> a profession <u>when</u> engineers improve their

*capabilities in the general fields of human endeavors.
When they learn to tolerate, understand and respect others
such that they can manage, lead, create, and inspire others
to a return respect and understanding.*

*Engineering cannot be a profession so long as it seeks to be
seen above the hordes by tearing others down. The term
Profession cannot be created by mutual agreement of its
practitioners, it cannot be created by passage of a law. It
does not exist in the absence of punch cards and hourly
rates. It can only be earned and deserved. Let's turn to the
task. How do you measure up?*

In April, 1963, Packard, Muir & Train celebrated its 10th
anniversary in business in Sacramento. Ten-year pins were awarded to
the founders of the organization–Luke Packard, Logan Muir, and Tim
Train—and to employees Art Roecker, Clint Calvert, Walt Arlt, Joe
Williams, and Harry Howell. The *Sacramento Bee* noted also that "...
the company's business volume [in 1962] *was $581,920., and its payroll,
$469,571. In 1953 they...*[Muir &Train and Luke Packard & Associates,
combined] *had 11 employees...Today the company employs 54.*" If one adds
dependents to the number of employees, the total number depending
upon the business for their livelihood was well over 200 people.

Logan was amazed at the annual company picnic when he saw all
the people dependent upon his going to the bank before each payday
to pay off the previous loan and take out a new one. In addition, the
bank always wanted proof of their work in progress and payments
received. With Logan's usual meticulous approach to any problem, the
firm's credit was good. But going to the bank to meet the payroll was
a draining experience. He didn't have to tell me when he had been to
the bank—I could always sense it.

Keeping ahead of the payroll regularly was not engineering. He
finally decided he wanted to be a consulting engineer on his own,
without the payroll to face regularly. In 1966 he left Packard, Muir &
Train and set up his own office on the Sacramento mall.

With Logan's departure from the firm, the name "Muir" had to be
removed from their title. For a long time they had been known around

town as PMT, and for the firm the name transition was easy. They became PMT Associates, and I believe the parting was congenial.

The news article announcing the new name also stated that the firm [Packard, Muir & Train, Inc.] was one of 26 Northern California firms to make *Engineering News-Record*'s roll of the top 500 design firms in 1965. It was the only Sacramento firm so listed, and won this prestigious recognition for the second time.

CHAPTER 15—THE BOARD OF REGISTRATION & CSPE
Resignation, Re-instatement, Resolutions, Recognition

Statesman, yet friend to truth; of soul sincere,
In action faithful, and in honour clear;
Who broke no promise, serv'd no private end...
– Alexander Pope

Appointment by the California governor to the State Board of Registration for Professional Engineers was, in the 1960's, looked upon as a prestigious honor.

First and foremost, of course, the engineer had to be known by the engineering community. When a vacancy occurred on the board, either by resignation or by expiration of the allotted term, the governor asked the engineering societies to recommend a qualified candidate.

Second, the person had at be good in his profession. The Board consisted of one member from each of the major engineering disciplines – civil, mechanical, electrical, and structural. [Since the 1960's the total number of engineering disciplines has expanded to make up the entity of the Board.] A good candidate would have naturally risen to the top in his profession and have a good reputation with other engineers.

Probably last in those days when politics meant government by the majority with due respect for the minority, if the candidate was also a member of the governor's political party, that might — but would not necessarily — tip the scales in his favor.

High ethical standards were expected without mention. Those were times of open discussion, but also of general trust, and people assumed that unblemished ethics were a part of the competence, with people of differing viewpoints still able to have a high regard for each other.

In 1961 Governor Edmund Brown appointed Logan to a four-year term on the State Board of Registration for Civil and Professional

Engineers. The Newsletter of the California Council of Civil Engineers and Land Surveyors printed his picture along with a brief biography, the last paragraph of which follows:

> *Logan Muir is a past president of the Western Association*
> *of Engineers and Land Surveyors and a past chairman*
> *of the California Council's committee on city planning.*
> *He has been president of Sacramento Chapter, C.S.P.E.,*
> *chairman of Northern California Section, A.C.S.M. He*
> *is a member of the American Society of Civil Engineers, a*
> *member of the Board of Governors, Engineering Council*
> *of Sacramento Valley, a member of Sacramento Association*
> *of Home Builders and the Sacramento City-County*
> *Chamber of Commerce. The committees and the drives he*
> *has chaired are legion.*

A few years later *The Sacramento Bee* of July 18, 1964, pictured Logan Muir with this caption:

> *Logan Muir, Jr., of the Sacramento civil engineering and*
> *surveying firm of Packard, Muir & Train, Inc., has been*
> *named president of the state board of registration for civil*
> *and professional engineers. He succeeds Dr. Carrol M.*
> *Beeson of the University of Southern California.*

And in *The Sacramento Bee* of January 1, 1965, this news item:

> *Logan N. Muir, vice president of the Sacramento*
> *engineering firm of Packard, Muir & Train, Inc., has been*
> *reappointed by Governor Edmund G. Brown to the state*
> *board of registration for civil and professional engineers for*
> *a four year term...*
> *Our state's 44,000 engineers require the most expert*
> *guidance and representation available to the board,"*
> *Brown stated... These members are fulfilling those*
> *expectations and I want them to continue their good*
> *work.*

The California Board of Registration headquarters were in Sacramento. Board members met one or two days each month at various locations in the state. Among many items of business were policy problems to address, bills to introduce to the California legislature, on-going oversight of registered engineers and policing of people masquerading with false registration. Logan came home from one meeting and remarked that the board members were among the finest engineers he had ever met. Just being together with them, hashing over agenda items, solving problems, was for him a stimulating experience.

Not to go back is somewhat to advance
– Alexander Pope

In the mid-60s the California Society of Professional Engineers (C.S.P.E.) wanted to take advantage of the newest computer technology. Keeping track of more than 20 C.S.P.E. chapters in the state, its members, its dues, and other office-type records was a burdensome task for an unpaid elected secretary, and could be handled by this new device called a computer, saving much time. The C.S.P.E. had no central office, and it sounded ideal to "put it all on computer" and get it done fast and right.

The member aggressively hailing the new computer technology had worked at the Jet Propulsion Laboratory in Pasadena. Though he was a registered professional engineer, it's doubtful if he had ever handled personnel data. However, with no C.S.P.E. central office and some members well aware of the time and effort involved in record-keeping, his idea was accepted as a way to better handle the Society's records. Subsequently, at his direction the information of each member was key-punched onto cards, the cards were entered into a computer en masse, and work-saving results were eagerly anticipated.

What evolved almost dis-mantled the C.S.P.E. Dues payments were improperly credited; members' names emerged in different chapters than their own; names were garbled; addresses were fumbled. Irate letters arrived in the secretary's mail daily. In short, it was computer chaos.

By this time Logan had left Packard, Muir & Train and had an office on the Capitol Mall. As a professional engineer with PMT he had given advice freely, always with the expectation of generating business for the firm. Now, as a private consultant his expert advice had to be purchased. Logan had time to think about many things, including the direction C.S.P.E. was heading with the new computer technology.

With Logan's membership on the Board of Registration, he was known state-wide in the professional engineering community, and C.S.P.E. soon asked him to be their executive director, part time. He would work from his home because they could not yet afford office space, but someone competent was needed to sort out the mess with the computer records.

Logan seemed to have a steady vision of distinguishing right from wrong. Some people sneered at the possibility of a conflict of interest with dual membership on the State Board and as executive director of a group registered by that Board. But Logan saw problems there. He accepted the challenge from C.S.P.E., and these letters to and from Governor Reagan were exchanged:

> *July 15, 1967*
> *My Dear Governor Reagan:*
>
> *During the past six years, it has been my great pleasure to serve the public of the State of California as a member of the Board of Registration for Civil and Professional Engineers. Recently, the California Society of Professional Engineers asked me to serve as a part-time paid secretary to that organization, a request to which I acceded.*
>
> *Although I do not believe a conflict of interest necessarily exists in my position on the Board and as a paid officer of a professional society whose members are regulated by the Board, I realize critics of the Board or your administration could well seize upon the situation and make issue of it.*
>
> *Since I would not under any circumstance cause undeserved embarrassment either to the Board or my Governor, I hereby tender my resignation from the Board effective upon appointment of a successor.*

*I am confident you will be quickly able to find an able
and respected engineer dedicated to service to the public to
serve in my stead on the Board for, indeed, California has
no other kind.*

Very best regards.
/S/ Logan Napier Muir

July 25, 1967
Dear Mr. Muir:

*This will accept your resignation as a member of the Board
of Registration for Civil and Professional Engineers.*

*I know you have been an excellent board member, and
I join with your associates in expressing gratitude for the
time and energy you have so freely given.*

*This brings you my best wishes for success in your new
position.*

Sincerely,
/S/ Ronald Reagan
Governor

Patience and understanding were required to sort out the massive problems created in the C.S.P.E. records. Our living room floor became the best place to spread out the huge paper sheets generated by this new device called a computer. Indignant members now had someone to ask why they were getting multiple bills; others wondered why they had been dropped from the rolls. The Director of the National Society of Professional Engineers came to Sacramento, stayed with us overnight, and wanted to ascertain if the California Society could get things straightened out.

With uninterrupted, painstaking efforts the names were sorted out, one by one, chapter by chapter. It took small persistent steps directed at each error to correct the C.S.P.E. membership list. But finally corrected it was.

With a brighter future ahead, the engineers wanted an office address and a place where the members could exchange ideas and create a stronger state-wide organization. C.S.P.E. rented office space across the street from Sutter's Fort in Sacramento and their activities were moved out of our home. Since I was by then familiar with the aims and structure of the Organization, I stayed on to assist Logan part time in running the office.

It was 1968. Arthur Flaherty, executive secretary of the Board of Registration for Professional Engineers, was preparing to retire and the board members were searching for the best possible replacement. Except for the newest appointees, the members already knew of Logan's abilities, and that he had served on the Board with distinction. On the other hand, Logan knew the Board's activities well, and when they offered him the job of executive secretary he readily accepted. He was by then a familiar name in engineering societies and his appointment was hailed statewide as a welcome step.

His office would be in Sacramento with a staff of about 30 people to help him handle registration procedures, examinations, complaints against registered engineers and licensed land surveyors and those masquerading as such, and the writing of proposed legislation affecting the engineering community and protecting the public.

During Logan's tenure as Executive Secretary the monthly meetings at different venues in the state continued, coupled with frequent speaking engagements and awards. My role behind the scenes often involved meeting him at the new Sacramento airport north of town, sometimes in the early hours of the morning. It was a long drive home through the north area and across the dam at Folsom Lake and on to our home in Lakehills. Logan was quite content to have me drive as he unwound from the stresses of the long day behind him.

Occasionally, if it was appropriate, I accompanied him to an event. One such meeting was held at Lake Tahoe, and the theme of "Miners and Dancing Girls" had been announced for the final get-together — a dinner-dance with everyone appropriately costumed.

Logan often used creative judgment — thinking outside the box — both in his professional and private life. For us, he suggested costumes of "Minors". I stitched up little boy- and girl-outfits in light blue. His had short pants with shoulder straps topped off by a sailor-type hat with a turned up brim. Mine had a short skirt with a bib top, a bit of white petticoat showing and, of course, a ribbon in my hair. As we approached the hotel lobby in costume, I wondered what the reaction would be. Hotel guests were used to seeing all sorts of attire, and there was little reaction except the occasional smile. But it was great fun at the evening festivities to see the Executive Secretary dressed as a little boy. Another couple borrowed the costume, and it may have gone on for several more lives — who knows?

Logan's creativity at work

And unextinguish'd laughter shakes the skies.
– Alexander Pope

At one engineers' convention in southern California, someone brought up at the final dinner what he thought was unfinished business. Most of the assembled group listened politely as several engineers haggled over some minutiae. The discussion dragged on and on. Logan could be patient when a situation required it, but this time he quietly concluded that this final relaxing dinner was not the place for business.

Our table for eight was a long way from the speaker's platform and we could scarcely hear the speakers. He and I were in adjacent seats and on his other side was the wife of a land surveyor who was as bored as Logan with the proceedings. Warmed by a bit of wine, she and Logan started to peruse the menu, then attempted to translate it into a foreign language — any foreign language would do, including a few which they invented.

With each new translation, their enthusiasm increased, until finally the crescendo of their laughter began to drown out the voice of the master of ceremonies. I was embarrassed, as was Jack Barrish at the podium. Still, how could they show him the door? He was there to receive an honor. There were other humorous events that evening, but this one ranked near the top.

Further honors were accorded Logan during his time as Executive Secretary of the Engineers' Board.

In 1970 The Engineering Council of Sacramento Valley

> *...cites and commends for outstanding service to the profession, 1969, Logan N. Muir, Jr., who is a founding member and past president of five engineering service groups; who was a member and past president and now is Executive Secretary of the State Board of Registration for Professional Engineers; who has dedicated twenty-one years of his life to improving the quality of engineering practiced here and statewide.*
>
> */S/Paul J. Reis, Chairman of the Governing Board*

One of Logan's friends was State Senator Leroy Greene, a graduate of Purdue and a long-time registered civil engineer. When Leroy was first running for the State assembly in the early 1950s, our family helped put up his campaign posters in the Carmichael area. Very likely

Leroy understood, better than most legislators, that proper engineering bills be passed by the California Legislature. In 1970 at the Engineers' Week banquet, Leroy presented Logan with a certificate citing him for "outstanding service" to the profession.

In 1972, when Board member John Winzler was near the end of his term, he sent Logan a letter, parts of which are quoted:

Dear Logan:

...While I am not known for my literary ability and I've never been able to properly express the kind and complimentary feelings that I have for others, I will use this letter to tell you what a helluva fine person I think you are.

Prior to your acceptance of the Executive Secretary position, I truly intended to resign from the Board in order to show my extreme dissatisfaction with the bumbling bureaucracy which the Board and its staff appeared to be entrapped in. Your perception and understanding of the political problems and your administrative know-how surely converted a most frustrating experience for me to one of great enjoyment.

While I don't believe any man is unexpendable, I sympathize with the Board in coming years as I truly believe you will be damn hard to replace.

What more can I say other than to wish you and your wife many years of happiness in your retirement.
/S/John
John R. Winzler

As retirement neared, other honors were awarded. On May 20, 1972, The California Society of Professional Engineers' annual meeting honored him at their installation dinner-dance. His Government Professional Development Award–1972 read, in part:

...Logan N. Muir, P.E., Executive Secretary, State Board of Registration for Professional Engineers, Sacramento, California... In recognition of outstanding contributions to industry, education, and government; service to the engineering and scientific community, leadership and pioneering efforts in development of new technical standards and procedures for the professional engineering sector. These activities have given new national stature and recognition to the State Board of Registration for Professional Engineers.

Clearly, Logan had come some distance since he attended his first C.S.P.E. Chapter meeting and was asked to clear the tables after dinner.

On June 13, 1972, The California Legislative Council of Professional Engineers presented this scroll to Logan:

WHEREAS, the purpose of the California Legislative Council of Professional Engineers is to support, develop, and protect legislation in the field of professional engineering and land surveying that will be in the best interest of the public welfare and safety and that will foster higher professional standards; and,

WHEREAS, as part of that purpose CLCPE stands willing at all times to assist the Board of Registration for Professional Engineers in any and all administrative matters; and,

WHEREAS, CLCPE cannot render such assistance to the Board unless there be adequate and effective communication, both oral and written, between the Board members and the Board staff on the one hand, and CLCPE on the other; and,

WHEREAS, there has been such communication during the tenure of LOGAN N. MUIR as Executive Secretary of the Board of Registration marked by greater attendance

*by Board members at CLCPE meetings and greater
participation of engineers in general in Board activities
than at any time in the past; and,*

*WHEREAS, there has also been, during the tenure of
LOGAN N. MUIR as Executive Secretary of the Board,
an improvement in the relations of the engineers as a
whole, including the Board, with the Administrative
Department charged with the housekeeping functions
necessary for routine support of the Board in its
responsibilities to the people of the State of California as
established by law; and,*

*WHEREAS, the California Legislative Council of
Professional Engineers, advised that LOGAN N. MUIR
would retire as Executive Secretary of the Board on June
14, 1972, did at its regular meeting of May 20, 1972, by
unanimous vote, adopt a resolution expressing both regret
at his retirement and thanks for a job well done, and
directing the President of CLCPE to prepare evidence of
same; now,*

*THEREFORE, KNOW ALL MEN BY THESE
PRESENTS: That the California Legislative Council of
Professional Engineers presents this scroll to LOGAN N.
MUIR, Executive Secretary of the Board of Registration for
Professional Engineers, 1969-1972, in appreciation of his
services and contribution to the public and the profession
during his tenure with its best wishes that he and his wife,
Ruth, enjoy a rich and rewarding life in his retirement
and the hope that he will, as time affords, continue his
relationships with the members of his profession to the
benefit of all.*

*Presented by CLCPE on June 13, 1972
by: /S/ J. S. Barrish, President*

And after Logan's last board meeting, another Board member kindly remembered Logan this way:

July 27, 1972
Dear Logan:

I apologize for leaving so quickly after the Board meeting in Sacramento… I wanted to let you know what a pleasure and honor it has been to have been associated with you these past thirteen months or so.

I don't think I have ever had the privilege of being involved with a group of men which performs as important a public service, or does it in as professional a fashion as does the Board of Engineers. We, as Board members, would all be kidding ourselves if we thought that it was due solely to the caliber of the appointments made by the Governor. I am certain that I speak for all my fellow Board members when I state that it is, primarily, the influence that you have had on the Board that makes it run as smoothly and as well as it does.

I have had the opportunity, in my very short professional life, to meet many administrators serving in many capacities, all the way from local service clubs to the chief executive of the state of California. I say, with all sincerity, that one meets a man with your talents for organization, diplomacy, tact and just plain effectiveness, all too rarely.

… you will be sorely missed by the Board. I hope, however, that the influence and direction that you have given us as Executive Secretary will enable us … to carry on in the same or similar fashion in your absence… my sincere regards to your wife…Kindest personal regards.

/S/Chuck
Charles R. McGrath

CHAPTER 16—THE SEARCH FOR UNCLE BOB
A Soft Scottish Voice

Hope springs eternal in the human breast:
Man never is, but always to be, blest.
– Alexander Pope

Logan's job often took him out of town for an overnight stay, and without fail he checked the motel's telephone book for Robert Waugh, his mother's brother. Logan knew only that Bob liked horses and that he went out west somewhere. The U.S. is big, and he could be anywhere out there. The chances of finding him were remote, yet Logan remained quietly optimistic and hopeful.

In August, 1961, the opening of the State Fair in south Sacramento was headline news. The *Sacramento Bee* pictured a trainer registering a horse for entry in the Fair's racing schedule. The caption identified the trainer as Bob Waugh. My excitement grew, but Logan was tied up with business that day. I told him I was going to the fairgrounds to see if this was <u>his</u> Uncle Bob. Andy and Al were in their early teens and went in the car with me to the fair gate where trainers and horses entered. When I asked for Bob Waugh, they told me he had arrived and where he would likely be found.

When we got to the designated place, an elderly gentleman was hosing out his horse trailer. I introduced myself, told him that Alexis was my mother-in-law, and inquired whether he was her brother. This statement did not seem to phase him, nor did it interrupt his work. When he had finally finished hosing out the trailer he said, *"I'll bet she's no chicken!"* At last here was the man Logan had been searching for.

Bob had a soft Scottish voice with a bit of a burr. He used few words, but his love of training horses to win always sparked his interest. We invited him and his wife Elsie and son Douglass to our house as soon as convenient for a reunion with Alexis.

It was a happy time as they all reminisced around the dinner table—where they had been, what they were doing. Soon they were talking about their relatives in Scotland. I was hard pressed to keep up with the family history and genealogy that unfolded before me. But my hasty scribbled notes did construct a rough family tree with names and personalities that were all new to me.

It was a delightful evening and clearly Alexis enjoyed it as much as anyone. Later when I talked to her about the event, she became aloof and sniffed, *"Bob never was my favorite brother!"* Though her obvious delight was hard to hide, she can be forgiven for the statement. Her "favorite" brother, Bill, was killed in WWI, and while she didn't openly dwell on that, neither did she forget it.

Bob and his family had a small house in Stockton, but the nature of the horse-racing circuit kept them moving from city to city as they followed the county fairs. They spent much time headquartered at the Alameda County fair grounds in Pleasanton, where they could keep a close watch on — and train — the horses under their care. Pleasanton is near Camp Parks where Logan was stationed during the last year of WWII. We didn't know at that time that Uncle Bob was a mere three or four miles away.

Before Logan's retirement we enjoyed the occasional opportunity to put everything aside and greet Uncle Bob at the races and root for his favorite horse. If Bob were entering what he thought was a winning horse, he would quietly pass the tip on to Logan.

Russ Markel was a business friend of Logan's and he and his wife had just bought a promising horse named Bal Rose. Logan introduced them to Uncle Bob who thought Bal Rose could be a winner. The Markels gladly turned over their horse to Uncle Bob for training. I was in the back seat of the car one day when Russ and Logan were in front. They were headed for Uncle Bob to check on how Bal Rose was doing. An interesting conversation was going on in the front seat.

Russ had never been to college but was well-known and successful in real estate circles. He said, *"Don't you think college sometimes interferes with one's success in the business world?"* All my siblings were college graduates and I pricked up my ears to hear Logan's reply.

"I couldn't agree more," he replied. He added that too many graduates think a college degree is the end result and they never have to study

again. *"A lot of people do very well without that degree. In fact some people do even better. Look at yourself, for example."*

Bal Rose was responding well to Uncle Bob's regular exercise and training. Understanding the horse is a crucial first step to good training. Bob said Bal Rose usually seemed to save his energy for the stretch.

We were in the stands the day Bal Rose was entered in the Director's Handicap. Excitement grew as we trained our binoculars on the horses coming around the final turn and down the stretch. Jockey Merlin Volzke said afterward, *"I was well back but was moving around the turn and veered to the outside when there was no room on the inside."*

The announcer's staccato recitation of the horses' names suddenly raised a pitch and changed to excitement as he shouted with enthusiasm, *"...and... here... comes... Bal... Rose"*. The horse went on to win the Director's Handicap. It was his usual come-from-behind, and *"...here... comes... ...Bal...Rose"* always brought a smile when Logan recounted the race to anyone willing to listen.

We had hoped Uncle Bob might go back to Scotland with us on one of our trips there, but he always shrugged off the possibility. He had come to the United States shortly after WWI, during which he served in France with a mounted section of engineers. Whatever the reason for his feigned indifference, we didn't push the idea, but always included him in family gatherings when Logan's Scottish cousins came over here.

In 1967 after one particularly good racing day in Sonoma County, we agreed to meet Bob and Elsie at his favorite restaurant north of Santa Rosa and there extend the day's happy events. We were unfamiliar with the area and Bob told us to follow him—he would lead us there.

At that time Highway 101 north out of Santa Rosa was a new divided highway. Traffic was light. We followed Bob as agreed, but he soon realized he had missed his turn-off. Used to solving problems in a direct manner, he simply bounced through the grassy, rocky median to reverse his course. With a healthy respect for the highway patrol, we thought it better not to do the same, but went instead to the next exit overpass. Some of the Scottish relatives with us at the time were either impressed or alarmed with Bob's solution to the problem.

On another day's outing Bob drove us up into the Sierra Nevada. We traveled on in silence, enjoying the scenery, except every few miles Bob would say, *"Yup"*, as if this were the concluding thought going through his mind. He was not an articulate man, but this brief expression of his gratitude for being part of Logan's family needed no further explanation.

He and Elsie occasionally brought fresh produce from a local grower — an entire flat of fresh grapes, or ripe persimmons from their own yard in Stockton.

After years of remaining in touch, we visited Bob and Elsie in Stockton as we had done so often. Bob was clearly showing signs of his 95 years, and had given up training horses, but was still able to share interesting stories of race track events. Finally it was time for us to go.

He stationed himself at the front door to say good-bye. He gave each of us a warm hand in turn and said in his soft Scottish voice, *"Thanks for everything..."*. Perhaps he knew something we didn't. By the next day his life had ended. But it was a good life — doing a job he liked best: working with horses. Relatives on both sides of the Atlantic were grateful that we never gave up the search to find him.

CHAPTER 17—OVER THERE
I've Come Home

From scenes like these, old Scotia's grandeur springs,
That makes her loved at home, revered abroad ...
— **Robert Burns**

In 1966 Logan left Packard, Muir & Train and needed some time off before setting up a private engineering consulting business in Sacramento. I had retired from teaching two years earlier. Our two sons were serving in the Navy in Viet Nam: Andy at DaNang with the Seabees and Al as an electronics technician on the aircraft carrier *Kitty Hawk* in the Gulf of Tonkin.

Ma was living in her own little home not far from us but was certain, several times, that she had been "robbed". She had always thought highly of her good neighbors and their two little girls, but now they were her chief suspects. The police were called and said we should take better care of her. The "stolen" money was always found — hidden at the top of the cupboard in a glass jar, or behind a picture frame, or in some other obscure place that almost defied discovery. She was "guy canny" about finding new places to hide her money so it wouldn't happen again. She even suspected us at times. *"Otherwise,"* she said, *"how would you always know where to find the money?"* Clearly, the time had come for her to move into our home where we could keep a closer watch on her.

"Keeping an eye on Ma" was easy to say but a daily challenge. She liked to walk and we soon realized that, after the door closed behind her, it was best to look out the window and see the general direction she was going.

Those were the days when sidewalks at intersections had high curbs and were not wheel-chair friendly with gentle slopes to the street. She didn't like the high curbs — *"...they shake me up,"* she said. She often admired colorful gardens and greeted friendly people along the way.

During one of her wanderings she had managed somehow to cross a freeway. How she did it is still a mystery. Ma was brought home by the local police at least three different times when she forgot to keep track of which way she was heading. But how could we put a stop to one of the few pleasures left for her?

Logan always had a yearning to go to Scotland and we agreed that if Ma was ever to return to see her sister Nell there, it better be soon before she became more forgetful.

The necessary arrangements were finally completed—passports in order; Alexis's clearance to return to the U.S. approved through the IRS (because she was a legal alien); airline tickets purchased; reservations in Edinburgh confirmed; Nell notified to expect us. The one thing we couldn't predict was Ma.

On the day of departure, Ma came down to breakfast, sat down at the table and said firmly, *"I'm not going."* What to do now? So many commitments already made, and Logan and I surely wanted to follow through with the plans. Logan grasped at the last straw of possibilities.

"I'll send you down to Dave—you can stay with him and Marcy until we get back." It was a desperate ploy. The mechanics of carrying out such a scenario were almost impossible. After several hours Ma finally agreed to go with us to Scotland.

We flew there on BOAC (British Overseas Airways Corporation), and it was a delight to be served by kilted stewardesses who asked, in soft Scottish accents, if we would like tea and oatcakes. In the seats in front of us were two older ladies who conversed all night, it seems, with a lovely soft burr in their voices. How could one sleep while hearing their soothing conversation?

The night was short as we headed northeasterly. The northern lights put on a beautiful show--just for us, we thought, as we watched the spectacle through the jet window. On this polar route we soon saw the early May sun appear on the horizon. It was easy to pick out Greenland, finally Iceland, and then western Scotland. What a magical world unfolded beneath us!

We landed at Scotland's new Prestwick airport in Ayrshire, where a warm Scottish welcome awaited us. Their excellent train service whisked us to Edinburgh, and from the train station we made our way to our accommodations near the west end of Princes Street. All through

Logan's life he had heard his parents speak of Scotland. Now he was seeing it for himself. He had heard just a few Scottish voices, been shown a bit of Scottish hospitality, and his heart-felt expression said simply, "*I feel as if I've come home.*"

For Ma, it was a little different. After sitting in the plane for about fifteen hours we went for a walk with her in the nearby Edinburgh neighborhood. We were a bit startled and knew she would need time to adjust when she said, "*This is the nicest Scottish neighborhood here in Canada.*" In 1905 It had taken weeks for her to travel from Glasgow to New York. Now, more than sixty years later the return trip to Edinburgh was only hours. Her confusion was easy to understand.

Our rooms were close together in the hotel, and the decision was to rest and meet for supper later—all in order to gently re-set our internal time clocks to the local system. When we knocked on her door at supper-time, no one answered. Was she still asleep? Was she out walking? Could she be having tea downstairs in the spacious lobby? A check with the desk clerk came up blank. No one had seen her. Where could she be? The clerk accompanied us to her room and unlocked her door to see if she might be there. When we found the room empty we knew we had a problem.

Nell was expecting to meet us in the hotel the next evening, and would come with a few relatives. What would we tell her? That her sister was missing? That she could be anywhere in Edinburgh? Was our trip in vain? Were we already too late in bringing her back to Scotland? So many questions. So few answers.

The hotel clerk gave us directions to the nearby police station where we reported Ma missing. They quickly assured us they would find her. "*Prince Philip is in town tonight, and she's probably in the crowd somewhere greeting him. Go back to your hotel, get some rest, and we'll know where to get in touch with you.*"

That was easy for them to say. We had a cup of tea at the local restaurant, and returned to our hotel room where we tried to sleep for a few restless hours. Finally at 3:00 a.m. we heard a knock on our door. It was the police safely escorting Ma back to our hotel. She came into the room, tired from her wanderings, and slumped into the nearest chair. After she caught her breath she blurted out, "*A bad penny always turns up!*" She had followed the street crowds to see Prince Philip, shared their enthusiasm, and very likely enjoyed the event.

One of the policemen took Logan aside and said,*"We found her in the toughest part of the city. Did you know she has two hundred American dollars on her? She could have been rolled!"*

Logan was as surprised as the police. Before leaving California we had supplied her with Scottish money, but we learned later that all of it remained in her hotel room, safely tucked away in the dresser. She didn't think she would need it *"here in Canada"*. However, we were happily relieved that she was found, and after "a nice cup of tea" we put another shilling into the room heater and tried to salvage some rest from the remainder of the night.

The next evening Nell arrived as scheduled. At that time her grandson George Scott was one of the few people in their extended family with a car. He brought Aunt Nell and her daughter Ella into Edinburgh from Bathgate. Nell and Ma had a reunion in the hotel while George drove Ella, Logan and me around the city to see some of the sights.

It was late at night, but sunset came late in that northern city in May. There was just enough daylight left to make the scene almost ethereal. George properly drove on the left side of the road (we still had our thoughts in the U.S.) while we eagerly looked up at the soft-lighted Edinburgh castle high above the city. They pointed out Arthur's Seat. From the car we toured the local area at more places than I can now recall—it was a quick introduction to Edinburgh, and truly a royal welcome for these first-time visitors. They invited us back to Bathgate where, for several weeks, more family members continued the welcome. They gave us two upstairs bedrooms in Nell's home.

Logan always said he wished he had had a sister, and here he found five lady cousins who treated him like a long absent brother come home. The picture of their only brother had a prominent place on the sideboard. He was among the allied casualties in Italy during WWII. It was also noticeable to us that there were, in the population at large, few Scottish men of military age—many had lost their lives in WWII.

Nell's trip into Edinburgh to greet us was one of her rare visits outside her home. Usually she sat in a comfortable chair in her living room, with the controls to the water heater on the floor beside her. The water heater was turned on only as needed and no one took a hot bath without consulting or informing her.

With so few cars owned by the Scots, vendors came down the street on regular schedules with their fresh fish, meat, and bread for sale. Residents went out to the street and bought those supplies from them as needed. Refrigerators were non-existent—or very small, at best—and fresh provisions were purchased for immediate use, not for long-term storage.

Nell's two daughters, Rita and Ella, lived with her in accommodations that would be described, in the U.S, as a small "town house" or "condominium", but in Scotland it was called a council house. Next door in the attached building was another daughter, Maidie, with her husband Dick.

We stayed with Nell for a week, often going out with George in his car to places of nearby interest, while Ma and Nell had tea together in Nell's living room. Gradually, after several days, Ma realized she was really in Scotland, and the lady with her at the tea table was her younger sister Nell. Ma can be forgiven for any confusion. Seventy-six-year-old Nell was a school girl of 15 when Alexis left for America in 1905.

One of the big events during our stay was a family dinner, with Nell's five daughters and their families all participating in the noisy banter, good humor, and general confusion. The dining table filled the entire small living room, and the plates of food kept coming from the kitchen, passed along from person to person, until all were served. After a week of this hospitality, we rented a car, partly to give them all a rest from us, and partly to see some of the outlying highland and lowland areas.

In 1966 hotels in the rural countryside were almost non-existent, but bed and breakfast signs in private homes were easy to find. It was a joy to stay with a Scottish family, listen to their dialect, and receive a welcome with a generous home-cooked meal and evening tea. At more than one such place Ma stayed up much later than usual because she was having such a good time. For her, the trip and the Scottish accents were beginning to bring back happy memories. For us, the rewards were in being there, discovering new sights and new vocabularies each day.

Before we returned to California, we laughed with them when we learned that their "cookies" are what we call "biscuits", and their "biscuits" are our "cookies". We raced each other up Knock Hill near Bathgate, laughing and stumbling all the way. I also had become rosy-cheeked like all the women over there who took cold weather in stride and walked wherever they had to go, no matter what the weather. The biggest compliment I received was near the end of our 1966 stay, when a clerk in Binn's Department Store asked me if I was Scottish (never mind Logan, who was actually the full-blooded Scot). It must have been my rosy cheeks.

We vowed to return to this friendly country so full of history, and anticipated the time when we could welcome some of Logan's cousins to the U.S.

And come they did. In 1967 Ella and Rita, along with their nephew George, came to Sacramento. It was then that we introduced them to their Uncle Bob. Another joyful reunion followed, with visits to the race tracks where Uncle Bob felt most at home.

We put all other events aside and showed them much of the state, from the Mexican border up into northern California, and from the Pacific Ocean to Nevada. This was the beginning of our "international" visits, which later became a focal point of Logan's twenty-nine years in retirement.

CHAPTER 18—A FREIGHTER TO FRANCE
A French Line Cargo Ship on the Oceans

Plough the Watery Deep
– Alexander Pope

In June, 1972 Logan's duties with the Board of Registration were winding down. We made the most of the next few months to finalize details as we anticipated a six month stay in Scotland. All preparations were going well.

Our modest house in Lakehills Estates sold quickly and we moved to a temporary furnished apartment in Sacramento. In Scotland Dick and Cousin Maidie had just completed a new house on a hill slope outside of Bathgate, and wrote that they were expecting us. We replied with fair warning: *"We're coming! And we hope to stay through the winter!"*

In 1972 freighter trips for passengers were not easy to arrange. Few travel agencies handled them. However, Logan had a friend at Travel Advisors of Los Gatos who was well-versed in freighter travel. His firm arranged for our passage on the *Magellan,* a French Line cargo ship that would sail from the west coast in August or September. It was scheduled to leave from Vancouver, British Columbia, stop in Oakland to take on additional cargo, and sail on to LeHavre, France.

At our apartment near downtown Sacramento our routine jobs were nearly completed. Logan had a few more speeches to give, a few more honoraria to receive, and we waited for news of the *Magellan.* With only a few details still to take care of in California, we anticipated an interesting and carefree way to un-wind from the busy schedules we had followed for a long time.

In late summer, on its northbound trip along the coast, we were told that the *Magellan* was going to anchor in the San Francisco Bay area for a short time where it would unload cargo, head north to Vancouver, British Columbia, and there unload its remaining cargo. After it restocked provisions and on-loaded its Canadian cargo, it would head south again, roughly parallel to the U.S. coast. We expected to get on at Oakland on the return trip. We learned later that our trip on the *Magellan* was one of its last Atlantic crossings handling bulky and varied cargo.

At that time *The Sacramento Bee* had a brief column of ship traffic in the Sacramento and San Francisco Bay areas—arrivals, departures, destinations. We studied it regularly, always looking for any word of the *Magellan*. To our delight one day the *Magellan* was listed under "arrivals". Armed with binoculars, cameras and enthusiasm, we hurried to the Golden Gate Bridge in San Francisco. From there we used our field glasses to scan the Bay for the *Magellan*. Finally, we saw "our" ship at one of Oakland's wharves.

"That's our ship," I squealed. We knew the docks were closed to everyone except those with ship business, but we used our binoculars and had a great view from the Bridge. My first lesson in freighter travel was presented that day when I finally realized we had no idea when the *Magellan* would be sailing for Vancouver. But our return drive to Sacramento was filled with excitement. We knew the ship was a reality, and we had had a long-range view of it.

Times in port are unpredictable. Freighters' arrivals and departures are not like passenger trains or airlines which cater to passengers on fairly dependable schedules. We, as passengers, were not the prime reason for the ship's itinerary, and were prepared to travel with possible delays and perhaps even unforeseen destinations. But we knew also that this was part of the delightful freedom of freighter travel. The travel agent kept us informed as best she could of the ship's itinerary and timing.

One incident almost threatened to cancel our entire trip. As Logan carried a heavy load of stuff to the car, he stepped off the curb unexpectedly and wrenched his back. What to do now? Would our freighter trip have to be cancelled?

A quick trip to his doctor gave some reassurance. Walking on the ship's deck would give him a chance for the best possible recuperative exercise for his back—much better than sitting still in a plane for 15 hours, which could stiffen his back and make recovery longer and more difficult. *"Travel on the freighter would be okay,"* the doctor said.

One day a telegram arrived. The south bound *Magellan* is by-passing Oakland, it said, and airline tickets to the Los Angeles area would be waiting for us at the airline's ticket office in Sacramento. We were to board the ship in Long Beach at one of the many docks there. Two excerpts from my diary tell of those last hours of preparation.

> *Tues., Wed., & Thurs. The last hectic disposal problems*
> *prior to vacating the apartment in town. Used up the last*
> *of food supplies. Thursday had dinner at the airport and*
> *picked up the tickets for Friday A.M. flight.*

> *Sept. 1, 1972. Up at 5:00 A.M. Hectic carting out of*
> *bedding and towels, clothing--all items used last would*
> *be thrown away. Really left too much to do for morning.*
> *Finally our personal items were all out of the apartment*
> *and at 5:45 A.M. we were on our way with our 4*
> *suitcases, plus a carry-on bag for each of us.*

Our first stop would be Al's home where he was waiting for us and would keep our car while we were away. He drove us to the new Sacramento airport north of town and there we checked our bags to Long Beach. The plan was to be in Scotland for about 6 months, so our airline carry-on luggage included only breakable items plus Logan's camera with its lenses and equipment neatly stowed in a firm case. I still felt as if we were merely going to a meeting somewhere in the state.

At the airport we mailed the rest of the "Christmas cards" to friends, informing them we'd be in Scotland for six months. Logan used a few spare minutes to check his baggage tickets once again, but one was missing. My imagination took over as I thought of the developing hassle if a bag were lost. My anxiety increased as I waited... some of the clothes in that bag were needed en route... someone would have to retrieve the lost bag at the airport... further problems filled my mind.

Logan didn't encourage my worries. He went back to the airport employee who had checked our bags. In only a few minutes—minutes that seemed like hours—the ticket was found, stuck behind others. My worry melted away.

The flight to Los Angeles was just long enough for us to calm down with a leisurely cup of coffee—a welcome rest after all the hurry and scurry. Our plane arrived at the Los Angeles area before 9 A.M. We hired a willing cab driver who studied his map and then drove us directly to "Pier C" in Long Beach. There was the *Magellan,* docked with a gangplank in place—our first close-up look at the ship that would take us to Europe. It was in the middle of a scene of wharf action, cranes and loading activity. We took a hurried scan of the outside of the ship that would take us all the way to France. All the way to France? I wondered to myself. I wasn't sure.

Logan climbed aboard and waited for anybody to show up. After a few minutes Lucien (Lu-shawn) appeared, introduced himself, and carried our bags to Cabin 3, which would be our home for several weeks. One of our first responsibilities was to surrender our passports to the ship's captain for the duration of the trip to France. As long as we were on his ship, we were subject to his care and orders.

Our quarters were a large two-room corner cabin with private facilities. Two windows (port-holes), built in twin beds, a dresser, 2 closets, and a full-length mirror. The accommodations were spacious compared with those for the same price on a cruise ship. Lucien called the shower "*le deuche*", and we knew immediately that we'd have to use Logan's high school French to communicate as best we could.

Our cabin door opened onto an exterior passage-way only a few feet from the water. But from inside the cabin, the open hold was just beyond our forward-facing port-holes. They gave us a chance to watch the ship-loading operations without being in their way.

The scene out there was all action. Yellow hard-hats were everywhere. The longshoreman in charge of loading operations looked like a pirate. He wore no hard hat but had a blue kerchief tied around his head to catch the dripping sweat. His ragged cut-off shorts allowed him to scramble nimbly around the opening to the hold below. He gave shouts and arm-waving instructions which his men interpreted: *Slow down! speed up! ... a little to the left! ... now to the right!* The crews skillfully managed cables, large boxes, bundles of sacks, blue petrol cans, and a few Hapag-Lloyd containers with sealed cargo. A huge redwood burl, with its awkward dimensions, was secured in a giant woven chain basket and lowered through the open hatch. A pile of animal skins and other items heading for European markets were gently lowered down the hatch the same way, and then disappeared into the hold.

The sign on the *Magellan* said we'd sail at about 1900 (7 p.m.). Dinner was advanced to 1800 just for today. We didn't want to miss the action and were on deck at 1930 as a tug nudged the *Magellan* away from the dock. At last the ship was completely turned around and gently headed forward. The water was beautifully calm through these activities, and we watched transfixed as the lights of Long Beach and finally the Palos Verdes peninsula faded from our site. Reluctantly we went below to our cabin.

My diary describes some of my sensations:

Sat., Sept. 2, 1972. I awoke to the slight rocking motion of the ship. It was like a cradle, only gentler. Creaking noises repeated themselves along the ceiling. They made for a restless night as I worried whether the ship was sound enough to make it all the way to Europe. Logan, the seasoned ship traveller, slept soundly. He told me later that the creaking noises are usual aboard ship, and they don't mean it's falling apart!

The next morning Logan finally woke up. We went upstairs on deck. No coffee until 8:15. It was a time for getting acquainted with several other passengers also waiting for breakfast. The large open deck for passengers was mid-ships. We resisted any temptation to lean on the railings – they were heavy with grease, a reminder that this was *a freighter.*

The Pacific Ocean was living up to its name and we were fascinated by the ship's wake which broke the calm waters. Near the prow were a few containers. Logan kept his camera handy for unusual sights. The air was balmy and enticing. Later Lucien brought out ping pong equipment and folding deck chairs with cushions.

So much to see. Land on the horizon to the east could be the Baja peninsula off Mexico. Our lives began very slowly to take on a kind of calmness as we looked out onto

the wide Pacific Ocean and heard the waves slap against
the ship outside our cabin door.

The huge dining area was on the second level. It was bright and cheerful with large port and starboard windows. At mealtime, to accommodate the ten passengers on board, two square tables were set for 3 passengers each, and 1 table for 4. The ship's captain with his first mate and chief engineer shared a fourth table. Jacque and Lucien served the meals. Lucien also kept our rooms tidy with soap and fresh towels, and responded to all of our reasonable requests with good nature. He is a black native of Martinique, with a wife and child living in Paris.

Besides Logan and me, other passengers included a young teacher from a Catholic school in Chicago; a young former auto salesman from near San Francisco, who was going blind and hoped to find a suitable less expensive place for himself in Spain, or possibly Scotland. An older American couple bound for Ireland was on board, plus a grand lady named May who was in her mid-seventies and travelling alone. Joan, a nurse from Toronto, had saved her vacation days so she could handle the vagaries of freighter travel and see some of the remote places of the world. A professor from UCLA was our table mate. He was travelling to England with a trunk full of books for his sabbatical year there.

Walter was the tenth passenger. He was a German who spoke no English, and understood very little of it. He was also the occasional source of friction among the passengers. Apparently he had caused some kind of ruckus in Vancouver, something the other passengers quietly spoke of with dismay and abhorrence. This happened before we boarded and we knew nothing first hand about the circumstances. Logan's and Walter's contacts were rare, but with Logan's usual diplomacy they managed to get along decently, in spite of the language barrier.

Altogether, it was a congenial group. During the trip we were often, out of curiosity, doing the same things at the same time. If anything exciting was happening on the sea, we all rushed to the railing to see it. Anything new on the horizon was a big event. Even flying fish took us to the window or the deck railing, and another ship in sight was a real eye-opener, with much speculation about its cargo, its destination, and which national flag it flew.

Sun., Sept. 3, 1972. A tour of the ship's engine room

at 4 was cancelled because of mechanical difficulty.
The Magellan idled in the water for 3 hours. The chief
engineer said there was water in the oil. The tour will be
tomorrow.

Cocktails today were served at 11:30 A.M. in the
Captain's quarters. There we had the opportunity to get
further acquainted with the ship's officers and the other
passengers.

Mon., Sept. 4, 1972. Today we watched at the stern for a
long time as the antics of numerous flying fish seemed to be
putting on a show just for us. They dove in and out of the
ship's wake in playful unison.

Everything about the ship was new to us and we were a curious group. One early event was a tour of the noisy engine room deep down inside the freighter. Chief engineer Sorin was our guide and gave each of us a pair of white gloves and a snow-white "handkerchief" to protect us from grease as we clung to the hand rails. We carefully climbed down several steep ladders, cautiously making our way deep into the bowels of the ship. Our instinct told us not to get our white gloves dirty, but we soon overcame that as we grasped each ladder firmly. Still, my footage seemed insecure as I tried to keep from sliding on the slippery surfaces. Logan was a more-seasoned traveler and seemed to know instinctively how to brace himself.

Down there the huge "screw"—almost as long as the ship, it seemed—and other vital machinery that propelled the ship throbbed constantly. Everything worked in unison to move the ship forward. It was a noisy and impressive sight. The heat was *intense!* One of the crew told us in fairly good English that he crawled inside one of the huge pieces of equipment yesterday to repair it. It was extremely hot and a fan was directed toward him as he worked. Without the fan he could not have done it.

As part of the tour we saw the "shop" where repairs are made; the shaft, down under, leading to the propellers; a spare shaft in case the main one gave out; plus other mechanical wonders. Now we learned where the muffled throb, throb, throb of the ship came from. If it stopped, the ship was dead in the water. It would be one of the chief engineer's jobs to make repairs so the ship could sail again.

Cool air is pumped into the living quarters by the air conditioner's compressor pumps, and gets to Sorin's apartment first where it is 5 degrees cooler than elsewhere on the ship. Part of the tour took us inside the red and black smoke stack. Within it is a passageway plus the fairly small, hot "working" smoke stack. During the tour we gained considerable respect for engineer Sorin and all the crew on board.

The next day we had a life boat drill. Everyone reported to Jacque for drill except Walter. We were fairly certain it was because he didn't understand English—or French.

Breakfast was served in the dining room at whatever time a passenger arose. The meal was simple and usually consisted of coffee with toast or a freshly-baked roll. Other meals were the high points of the day. For lunch and dinner three newly opened bottles of wine—white, rosê and red—were set on each table. The wine was an appropriate complement, and most table cloths had red stains from wines poured while the ship gently rocked. There was also plenty of time to pursue interesting conversations.

The meals were served in small courses as was customary in an elegant French restaurant. An appetizer, a seafood, a main dish of beef or pork with a vegetable, a salad, and a dessert of some kind, were each served as a small course, with plenty of time to savor each one. I don't know who was their chef, but the French take dining seriously and tolerate nothing but the best at their tables. Our freighter fare was no exception. I have never had better food anywhere.

The *Magellan* had two superstructures, one forward and one aft, separated by an open deck area where enough lounging deck chairs were available so that each passenger could bask in the sun. It was in this area, when we headed into warmer waters, that the crew erected a square swimming pool and pumped it full of sea water. The salty water gave extra lift to the body, and the waves, which didn't look very big in the ocean, were huge in that small swimming pool.

After several days we approached an impressive landmark, the Trans-America highway bridge. It links North- and South- America just before ships enter the Panama Canal from the Pacific Ocean side. Rain clouds were threatening as we huddled together under one of the Magellan's small covered areas on the top deck. We could have gone under cover inside, but didn't want to miss a bit of the highway bridge and the Canal just ahead. The warm heavy rains passed quickly.

Before entering the Canal area we were told to keep our cabins locked. Our captain would be turning over control of the ship to Panamanians, who would be coming aboard to guide our ship through the locks. In so doing, they would have the free run of the ship.

The newest ocean-going ships were built with the Canal's dimensions in mind, and each of those large ships nearly filled one of the locks by itself. Only a few feet, or sometimes inches, separated the sides of the Canal from the biggest vessels, and extreme caution and very slow speed were necessary. By comparison ours was a small ship, and we waited for the go-ahead until another small ship came to go through the locks with us.

The "mules" on adjacent tracks pulled the ship along slowly through each new basin. Logan and another passenger speculated later about building a toy canal system, complete with locks. It would be fascinating for a child, they decided, and at the same time it would subtly explain the engineering principles involved. They didn't build their model, but on the freighter there was plenty of time for speculation.

After about eight hours of traversing the Canal locks and then Gatun Lake on the Atlantic side, we emerged into the Caribbean Sea. The water there was bluer and white caps were whiter than any we had ever seen. Our passage took us northeast through the Gulf of Mexico near Martinique, Lucien's childhood home. When we sailed past the distant Dominican Republic, we were finally heading out into the vast Atlantic Ocean.

One evening after eating our last dinner course, the table was cleared for dessert and we all waited for the cook's latest creation. Soon the lights were dimmed and Jacque came to our table carrying, high above his head, a baked Alaska with candles flickering on top. It was my birthday. He stopped at our table, softly hummed a few bars of happy birthday, and we all celebrated the occasion. The freighter setting was lovely, the dessert was delicious, and I didn't mind being a whole year older.

Every midday the ship's captain prepared cards labelled *"Pointe Midi"* and gave each passenger one for reference. From the latitude and longitude on those cards, we could plot our course and progress on their big globe and map of the world. Our ship was only a small dot with what seemed like very tiny progressions across the huge bodies of water. But day by day we could see that the *Magellan* was making headway.

The ship headed northeasterly across the vast Atlantic and our days took on a kind of predictability. The weather gradually became cooler, the swimming pool was dismantled, and we continued to scan the horizon for other ships nearby, speculating where each one was headed and what its cargo might be.

During our passage the screw down in the hold developed a mechanical problem and needed replacement. Now we understood why a replacement screw was always stowed aboard. For about 10 daylight hours the ship was incredibly quiet– we missed the throb, throb, throb of the engine. The *Magellan* was dead in the water, and we knew some of the crew were making very important repairs below. Nothing to do but take a nap during that time, and when we awoke the ship had drifted completely around so that the sun was "setting" in the east. Finally we heard the throb, throb of the engines sputter to a start and knew the repair had been successful.

As we approached the English channel, we continued to appreciate the vastness of the waters. It was impossible to see land on either side, and it was a long time before we knew we were nearing LeHavre, France. Fog had settled in and a chill in the air told us we'd need our warm jackets.

Finally LeHavre was visible with its docks shrouded in light fog. The *Magellan* docked gently and we saw that it was anchored just behind a huge passenger ship: it was *LaFrance*, the biggest ship afloat! We marvelled that we had come all the way from California in the small freighter that was home to us for three weeks. But it got us to Europe and had been a good trip with just the relaxation we needed at that time.

The ferry to Southhampton, England, was docked nearby, but with our huge number of bags, we and two other passengers hired a cab to take us there. The small taxi was piled high with luggage and the professor's huge supply of books for his sabbatical stay in England. It was an 8-hour ferry trip before we sailed completely across the Channel and finally set foot on English soil.

The custom agents in Southhampton were waiting for us. Four men in their office didn't have a lot to do, it seemed, and we were welcomed with greetings and smiles. The U.S. had helped Britain during WWII, when the country was in peril, and no one over there ever forgot.

The agent wanted to know if we had any liquor with us. Of course we did. We were allowed to bring into the country two bottles of spirits and two bottles of wine. Nevertheless, instead of two bottles of spirits and two bottles of wine, we carried four bottles of spirits. The agent was congenial and in a happy frame of mind. He looked at our collection, and with a wink he loudly stated that we had two bottles of wine and two bottles of spirits. Leave it to Ruth (the teacher!) to pipe up and correct him. *"No! We have four bottles of spirits!"*

With that announcement the other agents in the little room heard everything, and Logan and our agent were in despair as they spent extra time filling out forms, paying duty, and other such things in order to let us into the country. It would be some time before I heard the end of that incident.

By late September the days were getting shorter and we would soon be in Scotland. Winter was coming on. We had thought always about the possibility of retiring there. Months of dealing with wintry weather and ordinary folk each day would surely answer our questions, and we went prepared to settle in for a long winter.

The wintry days gave us plenty of time to look over the country and, perhaps, even buy a house. One that we really liked had a small plaque on it that said it had been owned by Sir Walter Scott's son-in-law. However, we soon learned that their way of buying and selling property was different than in the States, with legal terms for such matters that were also different from ours. Buying property there would be a little like skating on thin ice—we might fall into a legal hole somehow. Besides, if we stayed over there, how could we show the cousins the U.S.? Our decision, then, was to go home and get ready to welcome them over the coming years.

In March, 1973 we prepared to go to LeHavre where a freighter would take us back to the States. The relatives planned a send-off. When the Scots all got together for a happy party in their homes, there was usually impromptu entertainment, as various family members each presented a "party piece". It was home-spun entertainment and was always accompanied by spontaneous laughter. Logan wrote the following poem as his "party piece" for our last get-together. He read it with a Scots accent and it summed up the good times we had during our six-month stay.

THE COUSINS OVER THERE

(With acknowledgment to the author of "The Closet on the Stair")

O dark the day and black the hoor when man first got the notion/That less than ane day wis required in which tae cross the ocean./ Such empty pride and arrogance has grieved my heart fell sair,/I mun bewail the leavin' o' the cousins over there.

The cousins over there, the cousins over there!/Wi' heathered feet sae nice and neat/The cousins over there!

Let poets sing o' peace and war and quaffs o' sparkling wine,/O' lordly men and ladies fair and chivalry lang syne./My muse is couched in lower strain; tae me sic flights are rare./Content am I tae sit close by the cousins over there.

The cousins over there, the cousins over there!/Such happy days I've lately spent/Wi' cousins over there!

'Tis sweet tae dream o' days gone by wi' yer lassie by yer side/I never took my lass a walk along the banks o' Clyde./ But hand in hand, we took our stand—a simple, modest pair/In Bathgate toon we settled doon wi' cousins over there.

The cousins over there, the cousins over there!/We drove them mad, it was so sad/For the cousins over there!

My mind goes back tae youthful days when we'd the right o' it./We didna' hold our fork in left when at oor meals

we sit./Our cars ran on the right side, tae, nae worry or a
care./Now clumsily we drive and eat wi' cousins over there.

The cousins over there, the cousins over there!/We're going
hame wi' heart aflame/Frae cousins over there!

There's some that cry for Tranter, and some that want
Shakespeare/And some that read McClean at night and
quake with constant fear,/But of a' they daft new-fangled
books, tae me none can compare/Tae a copy o' the <u>Sunday
Post</u> with cousins over there!

The cousins over there, the cousins over there!/Checking on
our coupons/ Wi' the cousins over there.

But now, at last, it seems that we must leave this lovely land/
And climb aboard an ocean ship doon on LeHavre's strand./
We'll sail doon tae tropics and breathe the summer air/And
mourn how it's still winter for the cousins over there.

The cousins over there, the cousins over there!/We'll miss
them sure, when ends our tour/The cousins over there!

The fishwife still keeps callin' up the street and doon the
close/An' the coalman still keeps roarin' selling slabs o' stane
and dross./And the horn up in the Caley still breaks the
mornin' air/But they've said farewell as we sail away,/the
cousins over there!

The cousins over there, the cousins over there!/We're gang
awa' tae bide awa' Frae the cousins over there.

But if this plea o' mine should fail and die through want o'
care/Then tae the Queen and Parliament, my lass and I'll
repair/And plead that in auld Scotia's realm, they'll keep
forever mair/A butt and ben for both of us near cousins
over there.

Oh cousins over there, oh cousins over there/Wi' yer haggis
puddin', Ne'er Day first footin'/We'll miss you all the mair!

[A few words of "translation" may clarify Logan's "party piece":

"*Butt and Ben*" is a small cottage out in the country, with separate livestock quarters attached to the house for mutual warmth in winter

"*Closet*" is an indoor toilet

"*Coupon*" referred to weekly drawings for winners printed in their *Sunday Post*

"*Close*" is a narrow accessable space between tall buildings, usually paved, with stairways worn and sagging from years of use

"*Ne'er Day*" is their New Years Day

"*First Footin*" is a Scottish custom of being the first visitor to cross a friend's threshhold in the new year. It usually meant bringing along a wee drink to share

"*Trantor*" *and* "*McClean*" were favorite novelists

"*Sunday Post*" was their Sunday newspaper.]

*   *   *   *   *   *

We made nearly 10 trips to Scotland. Each time we were welcomed warmly, with the use of their family homes and automobiles. Often we searched for genealogical information, particularly about Logan's father.

The cousins came to the U.S.—three generations of them in no particular order—and we always hoped they felt as welcomed here as we did there. To this day I look forward to the letter or telephone call that tells me some relatives from Scotland are on their way over here. I may not be able to accompany them everywhere now, but they are quite capable of seeking out what they want to see. I've learned to eat sensibly, as the Scots do, with the knife in the right hand and the fork in the left. That way I can keep up with them, although peas are still a big problem.

I can almost understand "broad Scots", yet they're quite willing to talk slower so I can "translate" what they're saying. A smile always comes on as I recall a recurring incident over there. Maidie's husband Dick sometimes noticed my bewildered look as their animated conversation sounded to me like a foreign language. Dick was perceptive and loudly commanded a stop to everyone's good-natured banter. Then he would point with his finger, and say slowly and very carefully, *"You Ruth ... me Dick".* Once again I was included in their conversations.

Afterword

The shipping industry had made an enormous transition during our six months' stay in Scotland. The Suffren was an all-containerized ship, and the only cargo visible from our cabin was a private sailboat, carefully covered in tarps for the trip, and located high atop the containers just outside our portholes. The sailboat became a kind of barometer for us, as we headed for tropical waters. The tarps began to loosen and flap in the winds. By the time we reached the U.S. the sailboat seemed to be intact, but only a mere scrap of tarp was dangling from it.

One drawback on the *Suffren* was that for the first few sailing days, until Santurce, Spain, Logan and I shared a cabin meant for one person. The cabin which *had* been assigned to us was occupied by a shipping company executive, who had priority. Our cabin-for-one was a bit crowded, particularly when we tried to fit into a single bed. At Santurce, the ship's executive got off, and from then on we each had our own cabin! They were forward facing and at opposite sides of the ship. Another passenger teased us about rocking the ship as we made our way between our two cabins.

The dining room on the *Suffren* was much like a basement hospital dining room might be. The windows were high and offered no view, and the square tables could hold four people. The food was excellent but mealtime was no special event.

The passenger deck was about the size of a 9x12 rug. Only six passengers were on board, but they were all congenial, for which I'm grateful. One couple was from England, and I am still in touch with their daughter and son-in-law. Another couple was from the Netherlands—the man had been traumatized from being held prisoner during WWII. They spoke little English, but we managed to bridge the language gap suitably enough to play the occasional game of Scrabble.

While the ship off-loaded some of its cargo in Los Angeles, we passengers had a free day on land. We rented a large car and took the other passengers on a tour of the high spots of the area, places they'd heard of but had never seen: Hollywood, Grummans' Chinese Theater, and other tourist spots.

When the ship docked later in Oakland, we rented a car again and took the passengers to some of our favorite places: Muir Woods, Twin Peaks, and other interesting Bay Area locales. We were on the Golden Gate bridge as the *Suffren* departed for the north and the ship's captain gave us a friendly "toot toot" as his ship sailed underneath. Our six months was coming to a close and we were refreshed and rejuvenated by the new sights and experiences in our travels.

*   *   *   *   *   *   *

Upon our return from Scotland in 1973, we needed a place to live. We wanted to be above the altitude where poison oak thrived, so we searched the nearby mountains for a suitable place. Alan had property in Grizzly Park, and we searched that area first. The elevation was 4000 feet. We found a little cabin for sale in that development. It was partly furnished, with six beds in the loft for the owner's six small children. Downstairs was a small bedroom, a living room heated by a fireplace, and a small kitchen area. It was almost new and, more importantly, it was above the poison oak.

Nearby was Capps Crossing Road, one of many roads serving logging trucks going into the El Dorado National Forest after the winter snows melted. From all standpoints, the little cabin was an ideal place. We made an offer, the bank carefully scrutinized our finances, and the offer was accepted.

Because we wanted to gather lumber from the National Forest we signed papers to agree to take only downed trees within our limit of 8 cords per year. We also agreed to fight forest fires there if necessary. We each had a chain saw and loaded up our little Ford Pinto station wagon over and over again until we had hauled home 8 cords of firewood.

Logan took his early morning cup of coffee up to a higher spot nearby where there was a huge stump of a tree long since felled. The view to distant Stockton was a marvelous place for contemplation, and the wild birds and deer enhanced the setting. That property was for sale. Logan pondered about buying it, but I had been reluctant to make further investments at that time.

Telephone lines had not yet reached the area and the post office was a mile or more away. One day as I walked to the post office to pick up our mail, a couple stopped their car and asked me, *"Where is the twenty acres that's for sale up here?"* They were referring to the land on which Logan's stump was located. The wheels of my brain started turning, my reluctance went out the window, and I hurried home to tell Logan of the people who were interested in buying "his" stump. It didn't take us long to hurry down to the real estate agent in Placerville where we made a down payment on the 20 acres.

Tom Porter was developing 3-acre parcels up there, and came to us one day to negotiate a deal. If he could include our 20 acres in his new Grizzly Park Estates subdivision, we could have any 3-acre parcel we wanted and he would build us a house. Logan insisted that in developing the subdivision, "his" stump would be part of our property.

Events were falling into place. Logan would have "his" stump, we would have a new home up there with a view, and we'd still be near the El Dorado National Forest.

Tom built us a modest new house on the hill and we lived there for another 7 years. By that time we had a telephone, and welcomed Scottish cousins there. During that time Logan did occasional civil engineering work for a friend from the Sacramento valley, and was called at least once to be an expert witness in Sacramento, where his deposition was given privately in the judge's chambers.

As we aged we knew we would have to leave our home in Grizzly Park Estates. Our search for a closer-in location covered much of the west coast from Long Beach in the south up to Port Orford in Oregon, for the best possible location. Each area had advantages and disadvantages, which Logan listed as an engineer would, in order to compare the locations. At last we settled on Vallejo, with the Mare Island Shipyard just across the Napa River from us. Though we were both in reasonably good health, we knew we would need to be near medical facilities in our later years, and Mare Island had the most promise.

Retirement gave Logan's active mind the opportunity to carry on with his dry wit and humor. When he received a letter from our auto insurance company, suggesting that he should consider their company for insurance coverage, he responded with this letter:

... Dear John: I just received your latest letter confessing that you had shut yourself up in your office so you could figure out why I haven't looked into your low priced auto insurance. Your efforts certainly paid off when you correctly divined that I was puzzled as to why you had contacted me for this special program.

Now, John, you shouldn't sit there locked up in your office all day because you obviously can't find out what's going on out in the world. And you don't have to punish yourself or do personal penance over this matter any more.

You see, John, for over a year I've had Policy No. 917-113-262 with Colonial Penn Franklin Insurance Co., although I never really figured out how the "Franklin" got in there. I don't think you ought to stay shut up in that room, John. You should get over next door to "Franklin" and find out what's going on in the last year or so.

Please do come out for Christmas because I want you to be real Merry and not sit in there alone with your thoughts about why I didn't look into your insurance offer. I want you to have a Happy New Year, too, out of that stuffy office.

Best wishes,
/S/ Logan N. Muir

P.S. Dear John: when I finished reading the first page, John, it said "over" at the bottom but when I turned it over, it was blank. Is there something else you wanted to ask me? L.

P.P.S. Dear John: I hope you don't think this is another of those "Dear John" letters and go locking yourself up again. Please, no! L.

On the last morning of Logan's life we walked on the wharf at the Benicia waterfront. We watched the California Zephyr on the opposite shore as it made its way along the water's edge headed for Chicago. In two days it would be speeding through Clarendon Hills, Logan's boyhood home. But Logan didn't quite make it back home alive. He stumbled onto a grassy area just outside our front door. As he fell he tossed his coveted walking stick aside and let go of my arm. He had previously told me, *"Don't try to hold onto me if I start to fall—you'll go down with me and you'll be hurt!"*

The next days were full of minutiae which conclude the final chapter of anyone's life. Logan's ashes were scattered in the Carquinez Straits, at a site where the waters widened out to more than 500 feet from shore. The former Navy work boat held six of his close relatives to do the honors. I think Logan would have been gratified that it was a former Navy craft and there was no big ceremony.

One of my duties was to turn in Logan's professional engineer card to the Board of Registration. When I made the call and told them my name and purpose, they immediately put me on hold and transferred the call to another employee. She wanted details of Logan's life and a copy of his obituary. The announcement of his death was printed later in the Board's newsletter.

Another event followed. Early in May, 2002, State Senator Wesley Chesbro of California's second district sent a large ivory-colored envelope. The engraved message inside stated, *"In Memoriam"*. I unfolded it and read

"𝕿𝖍𝖊 𝕮𝖆𝖑𝖎𝖋𝖔𝖗𝖓𝖎𝖆 𝕾𝖙𝖆𝖙𝖊 𝕾𝖊𝖓𝖆𝖙𝖊 𝖔𝖓
𝕸𝖆𝖞 8, 2002
𝖆𝖉𝖏𝖔𝖚𝖗𝖓𝖊𝖉 𝖎𝖓 𝖒𝖊𝖒𝖔𝖗𝖞 𝖔𝖋

𝕷𝖔𝖌𝖆𝖓 𝕸𝖚𝖎𝖗

The tribute was unexpected. Logan never wanted me to be sad. With clouded eyes I managed to read on:

"On behalf of the California Senate may I express our deepest sympathy."

It was signed by Senator Wesley Chesbro 2nd District

My thank you to the Senator follows:

1602 Spyglass Pkwy
Vallejo, CA 94591-6936
May 16, 2002

The Honorable Wesley Chesbro
Senator, California State Senate
State Capitol
Sacramento, CA 95814-4906

Dear Senator Chesbro:

I am deeply touched by the honor the California State Senate bestowed on my beloved husband, Logan N. Muir, on May 8, 2002.

During the 57 years we shared, I knew him as an extraordinary man who was a force for good in the business and civic world, and who strove always to solve problems with solutions that were both moral and ethical. It is gratifying to know that those outside our family recognize his accomplishments also.

Thank you for the beautiful tribute. His dear family will treasure it greatly, along with other mementoes of a great life, honorably lived.

My thoughts and very best wishes go with you as you move forward to help to solve the problems of the State of California.

Sincerely,
/S/ Ruth C. Muir
(Mrs. Logan N. Muir)

About 50 individually-composed letters were sent to relatives and close friends, telling of our last days together and, following Logan's advice, asking them not to be sad. *"Have a party, raise a glass if you desire, and remember him happily"*, the letters said.

www.ingramcontent.com/pod-product-compliance
Lightning Source LLC
Chambersburg PA
CBHW061252280526
45784CB00002B/736